GOETHE

S

CHARLES M. DOUGHTY, A CRITICAL STUDY

GOETHE

AS REVEALED IN
HIS POETRY

by

BARKER FAIRLEY, 1887-
University College, Toronto

Exclusive Agents for the United States
THE UNIVERSITY OF CHICAGO PRESS
CHICAGO ILLINOIS

PRINTED IN GREAT BRITAIN AT
THE TEMPLE PRESS, LETCHWORTH, HERTS
FIRST PUBLISHED IN 1932

PREFACE

THE English generation to which it falls to acknowledge the centenary of Goethe's death (22nd March,
1932) comes to the event with little apparent relish.
In the opinion of Mr. T. S. Eliot, Goethe "is at present
in eclipse" (see the *Nation and Athenæum*, 12th January,
1929), and Mr. Ellis Roberts goes farther and says that
"for Goethe most modern men, unless they are
Germans, have a positive distaste" (see the *Bookman*,
London, March 1930). This is not the whole story—Goethe
is too rich, he touches the modern world at too many
points, to be put in anybody's nutshell—but it would be
idle to deny that it is part of the story. And while
this is regrettable for those who care for Goethe, it
furnishes the author of yet another book on him with a
convenient apology. Far from having come to the end
of Goethe we are back at the beginning again. "It is
highly desirable," says Mr. Eliot, "that he should again
be admired and studied. But it is not merely a question
of reviving a reputation; it is, at least in England and
America, a matter almost of establishing a new one, so
completely must critical opinion be revised."

It is not my purpose to examine this decline of interest,
nor is it necessary to make much of it. When a few
bubbles have been pricked Goethe will appear in a
very different light. The not unprevalent notion that
because he was deeply admired by the Victorians he
was one of them, a remoter Carlyle or an ampler Arnold,
is amusing. If it is affirmed that he stands and falls
with the nineteenth century, it is enough to point out
that in his brochure *Kant und Goethe*, Georg Simmel,

v

his profoundest critic, has argued the opposite view con-
vincingly.   It is one thing to uncover the weaknesses
of Wordsworth's nature philosophy, as Mr. Herbert
Read and Mr. Irving Babbitt have recently done, and
another to uncover the weaknesses of Goethe's.   The
Olympian view of him sitting above our uncertainties
in cold and contented isolation has against it the overwhelming evidence of his poetry where he appears as a
problematic nature to the last.   And so on.

Perhaps the primary reason for the decline—doubly
unfortunate because we are better able to understand
him now than before, if we only knew it—is that we
have seen him too exclusively as a man with a message.
Carlyle's over-emphasis on *Wilhelm Meister* and the
moralist in Goethe at the expense of the poet and the
scientist has worked against him in the long run.   My
intention in this book is to shift the emphasis, as I think
it should be shifted, from the moralist to the poet, and
to work out a view of the poetry more clearly defined
than that which commonly prevails, at least among
English readers.   There can be no doubt that along
with the decline in interest a distressing vagueness has
settled on the name of Goethe—in contrast with the
names of all other poets of high and established reputation—and the fault is certainly with Goethe's critics,
not with Goethe himself.   When this vagueness   is
removed and his name recovers the clearness of conno-
tation, which it should never have lost, I think it will
be seen how close he is to our present aspirations and
how well he has anticipated those good minds of to-day
who are feeling their way towards a true science of
poetry.   They turn everywhere for assistance, save
only to Goethe, who perhaps has most to teach them.
I have not tried to argue this, but have preferred to
show the profile of his poetic mind—and therewith of
his deeper mind—and to let it speak for itself.

The book is addressed as much to the student of poetry

as to the specialist in Goethe, and in order to accommo-
date the reader who is unfamiliar with German I have
thought it convenient to give prose renderings or
paraphrases of all the passages which I quote in the
original. This has its drawbacks. Goethe, for all his
nearness to us in date and language, is among the most
untranslatable of poets, as the English *Faust* translations
show. I can only ask the indulgence of those who
have no need of my renderings. They are not always
as close as they might be; they are intended to meet the
need of the moment, to carry on the argument, and no
more. I am aware, too, that in quoting Goethe's prose
in English only I am putting it at a disadvantage.
Werther is notoriously a work which is sometimes felt
to be obsolete by those who know it in translation, but
which remains palpitatingly alive in the original German.

The remarks on Shakespeare in the last chapter are
put forward from the Goethean angle. They state a
view of Shakespeare which forces itself on me when I
come to him from Goethe, and as such they seemed
worth recording. I trust they will be read in this
spirit, not as some would-be absolute pronouncement.

B. F.

1931.

CONTENTS

Dass du schauest, nicht schwärmst.

CHAPTER I

THE APPRENTICE TO SHAKESPEARE

IT was as a worshipper of Shakespeare that Goethe made his *début* in European literature. The eulogy of Shakespeare which he wrote in Frankfurt late in 1771 and probably declaimed there to a little band of fellow-enthusiasts is as rapt a tribute as ever poet paid to poet, though, as he tells us, it was written without much reflection; he has not yet had time to think about Shakespeare; feelings, intimations, he confesses, are all he can boast of. These were overwhelming. To few generations of writers, if any, can the natural energy of Shakespeare have come with such a rush of release as to that awakening generation little more than a century and a half ago in Germany, which had Herder for its leader and Goethe for its greatest hope. Newly escaped from the dust of the old school, and especially from the stuffy dictatorship of Leipzig, these young men felt the impact of Shakespeare as a hurricane challenging the strong to stand up and face it, and driving the weaklings to cover. "The first line of him that I read," says Goethe, "made me his for life, and when I had gone through the first play I felt like one born blind whose sight was restored in a moment by a magic hand. The life in me was infinitely enlarged, I felt it most vividly" — words as conspicuous in the history of Shakespeare appreciation as they are vital to the biography of Goethe.

Both as a rhapsodic composition and as a document in the annals of European poetry this inspired address is to be prized and remembered. It is only when Goethe comes to put his inspiration into practice, and to give creative evidence of what Shakespeare means to him, that we have anything to question. Within a few weeks of composing the address we find him engaged in writing a play in Shakespearean vein, and a few weeks more sees him at the end of his short labour. The first draft of *Götz von Berlichingen* begins to circulate in manuscript among intimate friends early in the new year 1772. First the manifesto, and then the deed; first the preface —for such it is in all but name—and then the play. But it is impossible to read the two in this close conjunction without recognizing their marked disparity. It is not a case of the mountain giving birth to the mouse. *Götz von Berlichingen* is too good for that. But it is distinctly a case of the chairman overshadowing the speaker by announcing him in too eloquent terms. *Götz von Berlichingen*, let it be said, is a work of perennial charm, one of the really happy events in European literature, a joy to write and a joy to read. But it is not what Goethe gave promise of writing when he cried: "Shakespeare, my friend, if you were still among us, I could live nowhere but with you." Reading Shakespeare, he is fascinated by the scope and profundity of his genius; the grandeur of Shakespeare reverberates mightily in him. "His plots," says Goethe, "are not plots in the ordinary sense of the word, but all his plays revolve about the mysterious point (which no philosopher has yet seen or defined) at which our personal idiosyncrasy collides with the necessitated movement of the whole." And again, Shakespeare "vies with Prometheus, shapes his figures after him trait by trait, but on a *colossal* scale—that is why we fail to recognize them as our brothers—and then enlivens them with the breath of his spirit; he speaks through them all, and we recognize their relationship." Thus resonantly does he answer to Shakespeare when he reads him. But when he writes Shakespeare the resonance deserts him, and he speaks with a slighter voice. *Götz von Berlichingen*, as far as it goes, is Shakespeare, but it is Shakespeare of the relief scenes, Shakespeare with the tension relaxed, Shakespeare off duty.

It is strange. The poet in whom the seed of *Faust* was already set and who possibly began to toy with his *Faust* before the next year was out gives no inkling here of his power to cope with such a theme; with one exception—and that a notable one—the Shakespeare inspiration fails to extend him. Knowing as we do the depths that were ready or all but ready to be stirred in him, we cannot but wonder that *Götz von Berlichingen* should be so lacking in them. In this youthful apprenticeship of Goethe to Shakespeare deep does not call to deep, though the deeps are there. Sound where we may in the text of *Götz von Berlichingen* we soon discover that whether we judge it by Goethe's standard or Shakespeare's this is a work of surface, if not of superficial, qualities, a work which revels in pageantry, colour, bustle, hurly-burly—the spur, the tankard, the broadsword—and is content with these for their own sakes.

Historically—and leaving Goethe out of account for the moment—this is quite understandable. The new trend in literature, with its growing partiality for descriptive fiction, seizes on the element of fiction in Shakespeare, the story-telling out of which the Shakespearean drama grew and with which it so deftly compromised, and creates, or at least consummates, the modern prose romance. The medieval novels of Scott, the translator of *Götz von Berlichingen*, follow as naturally upon this early Goethe as Goethe upon Shakespeare. Nothing could be neater. Dramatic in form, narrative in effect, *Götz von Berlichingen* is the ideal link between the Elizabethan drama and the Waverley novels. The only surprise is that it should be Goethe who supplies it. For in doing so he put himself in what proved to be a

strange position. It was his destiny, as he quickly
discovered—he knew it for certain in 1775, and he may
have known it as soon as he was clear of *Werther*—to
hold aloof from the current of the times and go his
solitary way, and here he found himself for the moment
one with the current, drifting cheerfully in the middle
of the tideway. He was neither a Scott nor a Shakespeare, and he was to lose little time in showing it, yet
here at the outset he played the go-between to the two
of them, passing the torch from the one to the other.
In every way, save only in the spirit of defiance to
convention which prompted him to flout the unities
and write as he chose, *Götz von Berlichingen* puts Goethe's
readers on a false scent, heading them in directions from
which he quickly turned aside.

Seen in this light, the limitations of *Götz von Berlichingen*, its boyish outwardness, its lack of any real poetic
intensity, its failure to be more than a mere tale, are less
hard to explain. In executing this, his first great success
in literature, Goethe is not quite on his mettle, and the
whole of him does not get into action. For once, and
never again on this scale, he is at play when he writes,
and the spirit of play, the holiday spirit, descends upon
us as we read him. Where the scenes touch us, as they
do here and there and not always where we expect it,
they touch us lightly like a summer shower, while for
the most part we are living adventurously with knights
and peasants and gipsies in the sunset of "the good
old days."

There is only one sentence in the Shakespeare address
that fits the play. "Shakespeare's theatre," it says,
"is a raree-show (ein schöner Raritäten Kasten) in
which the history of the world is unrolled before us on
the invisible thread of time." It is an isolated sentence,
a little out of context maybe, but not otherwise perplexing. Like the rest of this address it is as much the
voice of the age as the voice of Goethe. It catches the

attitude to Shakespeare which came most natural to a group of writers who had just been roused to a native sense of the past, and who needed the chronicle play for their own purposes. The metaphor which sums it up, the metaphor of the raree-show, familiar as it must have been to one who knew the Frankfurt fair and its entertainments, is no exclusive property of Goethe's. It is a catchword of the times, and not at first sight significant. Yet trite though the phrase is, there is evidence that it meant more to Goethe than to the others who used it, and that it had a more precise meaning for him. It is not *Götz von Berlichingen* alone with its rapid scene-shifting—dungeon, taproom, palace, camp, highway, and what not—that makes us suspect this. There is also, to take an early indication, the little poem written on his sixteenth birthday, in which Goethe—prompted, it may be, by the rhyme, yet yielding also to a mental association—likens the aspect of the world among other things to "the minds of poets," and then, immediately after, to a "peepshow":

> Fast wie Köpfe von Poeten,
> Fast wie schöne Raritäten.

And there are Jarno's words introducing Shakespeare in *Wilhelm Meister*—the passage was written some twelve years later, and five years after *Götz von Berlichingen*— "You cannot spend your time better than by cutting yourself off from everything, and in the solitude of your old chamber looking into the magic lantern (die Zauber-laterne) of this unknown world." Coming as it does at the beginning of that part of *Wilhelm Meister* which contains Goethe's searching interpretation of *Hamlet*, this phrase is not particularly happy. One would not have expected it at this date and in this setting.

It is just as in the Shakespeare address of 1771. Along with Shakespeare the demiurge, working from the centre, Goethe sees the showman Shakespeare with

his magic-lantern. He has, in these years, a double
view of him and, with *Götz von Berlichingen* to help us,
we can see how he came by it. As a critic and admirer
of Shakespeare he sees deeply into him; putting his later
pronouncements with his earlier we can say that none
has seen more deeply; but as a poet, responding creatively to him and taking his cue from him, he stops at
the surface or near the surface. If Goethe were a
slighter poet or if his genius had been retarded, there
would be little call for comment, but, as we have noted,
the years which saw him following in the wake of
Shakespeare also saw the birth of *Werther* and of *Faust*,
to say nothing of shorter poems scarcely less profound.
It was only when Goethe worked in direct imitation of
Shakespeare, when he tried to catch his specific impulse
and become a Shakespearean poet, that he fell short of
himself and wrote, however competently—this holds
good for *Egmont* as for *Götz von Berlichingen*—as if he
were shorn of his mysterious insight into the heart of
things. This is what Herder meant when he returned
the manuscript of *Götz von Berlichingen* with the
unsparing comment: "It is all head-work" (Es ist alles
nur gedacht). He might not less aptly have said: "It is
all done from the outside," or even: "It is all done with
the eye," so visual is it, so deficient in inwardness.

The exception is Goethe's treatment of the character
of Adelheid. Of the other characters in the play we
can say that they are admirably sketched according to
the usual standards of an historical yarn, but we can
say little else. Götz himself, the great-hearted free-
lance, staunch alike in feud and friendship; Weislingen,
the turn-coat and ladies' man; Brother Martin, the friar,
manlier than his vows; the lad Georg, itching for his
first fight—these are as delightful inhabitants as any of
that select borderland of adventure which the grown
mind shares with the adolescent. But Adelheid is
something more. If Götz and Georg take us to Scott

and his followers and belong rather to simple fiction than to poetry, Adelheid, as Goethe first created her, takes us straight to the tragic drama and to Shakespeare.

It is distinctive of Shakespeare among the highest poets that he continuously has the power to create a character which is not himself and to let it go its way without losing his imaginative hold on it or relaxing the imaginative tension with which he first conceived it. We can apply this test to his major characters or his minor characters, to Hamlet or to Enobarbus. It is a feat which he has performed ten times to any other poet's once. Goethe's Adelheid is one of the few and one of the most exciting instances outside Shakespeare of this phenomenon. Unlike the other leading figures in this play, she is not taken from its historical sources, or from any specific experience or acquaintance of Goethe's. She is conceived neither in Götz's way nor in Weislingen's, but is pure imagination, as we commonly put it, a creature who owes nothing definite to any predecessor in life or literature. Any pedigree she may be suspected of having links her with Shakespeare's figures, with Lady Macbeth or with Cleopatra, compared with whom she partly makes up in swift demoniacal power for what she undeniably lacks in richness and depth of character. Adelheid is simply and forcefully conceived as the adventuress and man-killer of popular tradition, masculine in her ruthless ambition, feminine in her devices.

She appears early in the plot as the courtly rival of Marie von Berlichingen for the craven hand of Weislingen, and she plays her part with due restraint until the close of the fourth act. But with the opening of the fifth she assumes command, and henceforth she dominates the action, and dominates it so well that the death of Götz in the last scene presents itself rather as a soothing epilogue to Adelheid's orgy of violence than as the protagonist's farewell

that it is intended to be. Beginning with the gipsy
scene, where in an atmosphere charged with supernatural potency Adelheid's seductiveness is fully revealed
for the first time, Goethe is carried away by her and
grossly neglects Götz and his business as a chronicler and
a dramatist. He now devotes himself almost exclusively
to Adelheid, who, in a rapid series of scenes, in which
in wavelike succession anticipations of the early *Faust*
alternate with echoes of *Macbeth*, ruthlessly makes her
way by means of sorcery and the feminine arts over the
bodies of Franz and Weislingen, only to be thwarted
in her ambition at the last. For the secret court sends
betimes its avenging emissary, who duly executes its
sentence of death upon her, though not before she has
first softened him to the point of seduction, and then
stabbed him with his own dagger.

The vehemence of these scenes is not soon forgotten.
It is here if anywhere in Goethe that we shall find the
true Elizabethan *furor*. Franz's words to Adelheid are
such as Faustus might have uttered in his first youth.
"How I detest the day! Would that we lay in primal
darkness ere the light was born. Oh, on your bosom I
should be one of the ever-living gods who dwelt in
brooding warmth of love, and gave birth to the seeds of a
thousand worlds at once, and felt at once the rapturous
fire of them all." And with a truly Shakespearean
abandonment he cries: "For the first time in my life
I know what it is to hope. The rest was but the
intimations of a mole" (Das andre waren Maulwurfs
Ahndungen).

The Adelheid episode—as originally executed by
Goethe in the fifth act of his first version—carries us
into the deeps of the poetic life. Here at least in this
quasi-Shakespearean play we sense a Shakespearean
excitement. The creator of Adelheid, we exclaim, might
continue thus for a lifetime, surrendering to one compelling birth of the imagination after another, till his

gallery was full. But this is not what happened. Goethe never worked again in this vein of self-abandonment to a visioned creature not himself, and even this promising excursion was sacrificed by him in the interest of the plot. In the revised *Götz von Berlichingen* of 1773 Adelheid is a shadow of her former self; Götz holds the foreground to the last; the best and worst of the play has been skilfully excised.

Whether Herder with his "Shakespeare has ruined you" was referring to these scenes or merely to the general looseness of the play, he was probably all in favour of sacrificing Adelheid and of knitting the structure more closely. But it is possible that in giving up what was truly Shakespearean in his play for the sake of what was only lightly so, Goethe was acting on a deeper impulse. When we consider his astonishing insight from the beginning into all that concerned his inner development, we may conjecture that he foresaw even at so early a date that this kind of poetic creativeness was not to be his, and that he cancelled his one reckless adventure in it by an act of instinctive self-discipline. But whatever the wisdom, the immediate profit is doubtful. The revised play gains obviously in uniformity, but it is poorer in content by the loss of an episode which, if it threw it out of all shape, also converted it for the time being from a dramatic picture-show into a dramatic vision of the heart and the passions.

One mark of Shakespeare is signally lacking. It is the Shakespearean kind of language, which Goethe, as a born master of language and, when he chose, a great assimilator of styles, might have been expected to recapture. To be sure, the play has obvious echoes of *Macbeth*, and it makes some lively play with Shakespearean conceits, as when Selbitz in the thick of a skirmish shouts: "Follow me! They shall cry to their hands: multiply yourselves" (Mir nach! Sie sollen zu ihren Händen rufen: multipliziert euch)—but this is more parody than anything and scarcely to be taken solemnly.   It is *Götz von Berlichingen* at its lightest and tells us little either of Shakespeare's verbal genius or Goethe's.   Of the profounder mastery of words the prose of *Götz von Berlichingen* has nothing to show; we shall search its pages in vain for the metaphorical splendour which is Shakespeare's.   If Goethe catches this splendour anywhere it is not here, but in short flights of verse and, best of all, in "Willkommen und Abschied," the most energetic of his Strassburg lyrics, written in the first flush of that awakening of which *Götz von Berlichingen* is a slightly later and more sophisticated expression.   "My heart beat loud, then quick to horse, on the instant.   Evening lulled the earth, and night hung on the hills.   The oak-tree stood in its garb of mist like a towering giant, where darkness with a hundred eyes watched from the thickets":

> Es schlug mein Herz, geschwind zu Pferde!
> Es war getan fast eh' gedacht.
> Der Abend wiegte schon die Erde,
> Und an den Bergen hing die Nacht.
> Schon stand im Nebelkleid die Eiche,
> Ein aufgetürmter Riese, da,
> Wo Finsternis aus dem Gesträuche
> Mit hundert schwarzen Augen sah.

This is the first stanza in its slightly revised but more familiar form.   Here, if anywhere in Goethe's lyrical verse, we experience the swiftly dissolving metaphors that we expect from a supremely gifted poet who has taken Shakespeare for his master.   Darkness rocks the earth to sleep, hangs upon the hill-side, clothes the oak-tree, and peers with a hundred eyes, and so on.   All is suggestiveness and shifting imagery.   It is metaphorical poetry at its happiest.   But it is not sustained; as the poetic outburst spends itself the metaphors recede and the manner imperceptibly changes till in the final stanza we find

only the barest and directest of lines. "But alas, soon
with the rising sun my heart is wrung at leaving. What
joy in your kisses, what pain in your looks! I went,
you stood with downcast eye and weeping saw me go.
And yet, ye gods, what joy to love and be loved!"

> Doch ach! schon mit der Morgensonne
> Verengt der Abschied mir das Herz:
> In deinen Küssen welche Wonne!
> In deinem Auge welcher Schmerz!
> Ich ging, du standst und sahst zur Erden,
> Und sahst mir nach mit nassem Blick;
> Und doch, welch Glück! geliebt zu werden,
> Und lieben, Götter, welch ein Glück!

Thus the poem passes from night to morning and
passes also from the veils of metaphor to the clear light
of reality. Yet such is its spontaneity that the shift
in its verbal fashion from richness to bareness is either
not felt, or is at once accepted as intensifying the
expression of a vivid passage of emotional life. The
poet does not in this instance live in metaphor, but he
comes trailing a cloud of it, and if we are quick enough
we see it dissolve.

This is one hint among others of the inevitable movement of Goethe's genius away from Shakespeare. It is
perhaps as subtle and spontaneous as any. But for a
broader hint we may go to *Egmont*, in which for a second
and last time Goethe essays the Shakespearean history-
play. Here, as in *Götz von Berlichingen*, the pervasive
reminiscences of Shakespeare are soon noticed. But
there is an important difference. When Goethe wrote
Götz von Berlichingen he allowed a genuine Shakespearean
impulse to obtrude itself upon a superficial one; the
workmanship of the play suffered in the first draft because Goethe's mind was moving towards Shakespeare
as he wrote. In *Egmont* we can detect it moving away
from Shakespeare. And again the play suffers.

We have the testimony of Goethe's autobiography

that the writing of *Egmont* began to occupy him during
his last weeks in Frankfurt.   And we have excellent
reasons for accepting the testimony.   Goethe was then
at the chief turning-point of his life.   If he had decided
to stay at home, marry Lili Schönemann, and consolidate
the fame he had already won, neither he nor German
Literature would be what they are.   This he must have
vaguely foreseen, and the strain was acute.   It was
during this great crisis which ended in his departure for
Weimar, that he arrived at his favourite conception of
the inalterable.   He called it "the demonic" (das
Dämonische), meaning that force in us which acts like
destiny, but operates within our personalities, and at
supreme moments overrules our wavering volitions and
carries us with it.   This was one of his deepest con-
victions, and it remained with him through life.   His
final statement of it in poetic form, written in 1817, says
that "man cannot deviate from the law of his being laid
down by the constellations at his birth, that there is no
escape from himself, and that sibyls and prophets have
said it":

> Wie an dem Tag, der dich der Welt verliehen,
> Die Sonne stand zum Grusse der Planeten,
> Bist alsobald und fort und fort gediehen
> Nach dem Gesetz, wonach du angetreten.
> So musst du sein, dir kannst du nicht entfliehen,
> So sagten schon Sibyllen, so Propheten.

Its earliest formulation comes from the lips of Egmont,
whom Goethe's genius, responsible only to itself, has
converted from the Dutch Stadtholder and paterfamilias
that he was into a preternaturally sanguine spokesman
of the demonic.   The incongruity between this modern
conception of the individual and a documented picture
of the Netherlands in the sixteenth century is patent,
and Goethe's resources were unequal to the task of
concealing it.   His technical failure is manifest at the
close of the play, which is in open conflict with the rest.

Beginning with excellent folk-scenes, partly modelled on *Julius Cæsar*, and presenting an historical background more carefully studied than Lessing would have required, the play finally concentrates upon a situation which has little need of these preliminaries. Everything hinges at last on the unhistorical and incredible optimism of Egmont, who, finding his head in the lion's jaws, decides in obedience to the law of his nature to leave it there, and leaves it there too long—a thoroughly uncomfortable and undramatic situation. The play ends, as Schiller immediately saw, in an operatic stalemate, Egmont soliloquizing to incidental music before being led to the scaffold, a victim to the tragic possibilities latent in the demonic temperament.

The intimate association of Egmont's temperament with that of the poet who made him owes nothing to conjecture. The famous outburst of Egmont's in Act II, which first announces his impassioned belief in his destiny, lead it wheresoever it may, are the words which Goethe selected a generation later to close his autobiography. As the autobiography closes at the moment of his departure for Weimar and he takes over the words of Egmont unchanged to punctuate the climax, there is no more to be said. It would be impossible to tell us more plainly that at this moment of his life he is Egmont. Moreover, this intrusion of himself shows so clearly in the text that even if he had told us nothing we could find all the evidence we need. The break in the play at the critical moment of Egmont's outburst; the iambic verse-rhythms leaping into the conversational prose; the sudden access of excitement, not fully accounted for by the situation; the temporary shifting of the whole work from an outer world to an inner— all this would tell us in no uncertain tones that something had happened. The passage sticks out from its dramatic context; it jolts us on what seemed a smooth road; so that when Egmont, forgetting time and place, vents his inner mood without reserve and cries: "I have gone far and I can, I must, go farther. I feel hope in me and courage and strength. I have not reached the summit of my growth and, when I reach it, I wish to stand firm, not trembling" (Ich stehe hoch, und kann und muss noch höher steigen; ich fühle in mir Hoffnung, Mut und Kraft. Noch hab' ich meines Wachstums Gipfel nicht erreicht, und steh' ich droben einst, so will ich fest, nicht ängstlich stehen), we are tempted to exclaim with Mephistopheles: "Pull yourself together and remember your part."

But it is too late. From now on the play is a compromise between a dramatic intention and a lyrical impulse that has overtaken it and brought it to a standstill. In some respects it is a surprisingly successful compromise, but a compromise it remains, and the play is the worse for it. The finest scene that follows, that in which Klärchen heroically pleads with the townsfolk to stand by her in an effort to rescue Egmont —a scene which for stirring dramatic appeal may be put first among all Goethe's writings—loses more than it gains by its stationary context. If we were able to associate it with the heroic and popular Egmont of the opening of the play instead of the introspective Egmont of the close, it would be twice as telling. And this applies to Klärchen's death also, which in the deeper life of the work gives no support to Egmont's death and is not supported by it. She goes her way and he goes his; they move on different planes and have to be taken separately. Whatever unity the play had in its opening scenes it entirely forfeits in the closing ones.

Whether this confusion in *Egmont* arose, as we have assumed, in the process of writing or was inherent in the initial conception is a question which cannot be answered outright, but it will scarcely be doubted, in default of absolute proof, that Goethe began the play for its own sake, as he had begun *Götz von Berlichingen*, and only thrust himself and his personal mood on it afterwards. For why, if he began with a clean sheet, should he choose Egmont for his mouthpiece—a character whom, as the facts show and as he tells us himself, he had to transform completely before he could use him, and who in any event moved in a world singularly foreign to his demonic idea? It would be unlike Goethe to choose so clumsily, where he of all poets was an adept at choosing well. If, on the other hand, he had *Egmont* already under way as a runner-up to *Götz von Berlichingen*, more solidly conceived and more earnest in tone, everything falls into place—the careful historical groundwork, the superimposed psychology; the realism of the start, and the lyricism of the finish.

Evidently there was an interference in the development of *Egmont*, just as there was, originally, in *Götz von Berlichingen*. Twice Goethe set out to write an historical play with a mind filled full of Shakespeare— the echoes of Shakespeare are almost as numerous in *Egmont* as in *Götz von Berlichingen*—and twice he failed to be consistent. In each case he maintained a general level of character-drawing, dialogue, and historical colour worthy of the best of Shakespeare's followers, if not quite worthy of the best in himself, and in each case something happened to throw him out of gear and disarrange his work. But here the similarity stops. In the interests of play-making, where the test is one of success and failure rather than of creative origins, it may be no matter whether a character which upsets the play comes imaginatively, from nowhere, so to speak— like Adelheid—or autobiographically, from experience —like Egmont. But it is all-important for the understanding of the poetic life. In the difference between these two ways of creating a character or conceiving a play, the empirical way and the imaginative, lies much of the difference between Goethe and Shakespeare.

In the earlier experiment, when he was younger in poetry and Shakespeare was all in all, Goethe managed, on the whole, to obey his master and stay outside his characters, but even here the personal note enters and leaves its mark — inconspicuously — in the figure of Weislingen. Weislingen, it is true, is so excellent a foil to Götz, shifty where Götz is true, and effeminate where he is manly, that if we read the play without the commentaries, he seems quite of a piece with the others, being just the contrasting sort of recreant that the teller of heroic romances would be likely to invent. And it is possible that Goethe did invent him in this spirit. But as he hinted more than once—in a letter to Salzmann shortly after *Götz von Berlichingen* was written, and again in his autobiography forty years later—he connected Weislingen with an episode in his own life. The broken bond with Friederike Brion, whom he was making love to at Sesenheim in the summer of 1771, was still poignantly in his memory when he came to *Götz von Berlichingen* at the end of the year. And while this Sesenheim affair was not one of Goethe's shattering experiences, and his dwelling on it was more quixotic than desperate, it was acute enough to require an outlet. Hence the little group of renegade lovers, of whom Weislingen happens to be the eldest. Seeing that Goethe followed in 1774 with *Clavigo*, a tragedy devoted exclusively to the Weislingen theme of infidelity, it was clearly on the cards that the theme might have asserted itself uncomfortably in *Götz von Berlichingen*, much as the demonic theme asserted itself in *Egmont*.

But in those weeks of enthusiasm the sway of Shakespeare was too potent, too intoxicating. Onward the young apprentice goes with his easy scene-making. He puts Weislingen and Marie into the picture—a limb of himself, as it were—but, having done so, he quickly withdraws from them, leaving them barely a drop of his life-blood, and letting them sink lightly into the tonality of the whole.   In the end it is not Weislingen who throws the play out of focus, but Adelheid, who belongs to another world.   Weislingen may have first suggested her, for some such figure was clearly needed to ensure his infidelity and make it plausible, but this is a purely dramatic consideration and does not involve Goethe's private feelings.   He shows by the sovereign way he deals with Adelheid that his imagination is free for once from all moral commitments.

If Goethe had been able to achieve the imaginative absorption in all his characters that he suddenly began to achieve in Adelheid, he would have written as Shakespeare wrote, not just as an imitator of him. If the whole life of the play could have seized him and possessed him, as this adventuress did, making him forget his peep-show and its local colour in some richer act of creation, putting him mysteriously at the back of his scenes and on every side of them at one and the same moment, and enabling him to work in the round instead of the flat, he would have learned all that Shakespeare had to teach him.   But this was a cup which he was allowed to taste, not to quaff.   He could sample the deeper Shakespearean way of poetry, and did sample it excitedly for a brief while, but he could not sustain the experience and make a play.   Compared with a Shakespeare tragedy Adelheid is but a flash in the pan, gone before we have had time to look at her. And, once lost, the excitement, the peculiar excitement, never returned.   Not in *Götz von Berlichingen*, and not in *Egmont*.   And the rest is un-Shakespearean.   No doubt there are masterly delineations in these plays, especially among the common folk in *Egmont*.   There is Klärchen, the light-hearted and fearless, giving everything to her lover, and ready to lose all in the end; there is her querulous mother; there is Vansen, the gossip and demagogue.   But unlike all that Adelheid promised and unlike what Shakespeare achieved as often as he

c

chose, these figures seem more observed than imagined, they belong—even Klärchen—to fiction rather than to poetic drama. *Egmont* gave Goethe every opportunity to show his command of Shakespeare—even in the first stages of writing he was appreciably older and maturing rapidly as a poet—but for all its merits it only confirms our reading of *Götz von Berlichingen*.

This is not the whole story of Goethe's relation to Shakespeare. There follow the Shakespeare discussions in *Wilhelm Meister*, the productions of Shakespeare at the Weimar theatre, and the late pronouncements in *Eckermann* and elsewhere—all deeply interesting and indispensable to the student of Shakespeare. The essay, "Shakespeare und kein Ende," written at the time when Goethe, tired at last of the wear and tear of stage-productions, turned from Shakespeare the playwright to Shakespeare the poet, must rank with the best of Shakespeare criticism. In intrinsic worth it far exceeds his youthful impressions. But it throws a less immediate light on himself, because it comes from his detached and appreciative mind and does not involve his poetic instincts directly. The peculiar value of his first reactions to Shakespeare lies in the fact that he is so close to him; that he is at his mercy; and that at certain times he can only see in him what he is capable of extracting from him for his own creative purposes. Even his early analysis of *Hamlet*, though it is incorporated in a novel, is criticism clothed only in the thinnest disguise of fiction; Goethe is already reaching the point of detachment and can hold his author at arm's length. But the Shakespeare comment hidden away in *Götz von Berlichingen* and *Egmont* is, for the most part, involuntary, and it tells us more about Goethe's relation to Shakespeare, poet to poet, than a whole library of his conscious judgments.

What it tells us is that Goethe was not a Shakespeare, and that he did not respond profoundly to the Shake-

spearean impulse.   Much as he worshipped Shakespeare
and endeavoured to follow him in his younger years, he
was never able to do so quite successfully; he was never
able to give expression in this way to the real depth and
originality of his genius.   All he could do was to show
that if he had chosen he might have become an historical
dramatist like Schiller, or an antiquarian novelist like
Scott, for it is with these, his younger contemporaries
and partial followers, rather than with Shakespeare
that *Götz von Berlichingen* and *Egmont* naturally range
themselves.   The affinity of these plays with Shakespeare
is a surface affinity; they take us rather to the histories
than to the tragedies, to *King John* or *Henry V*, it may
be, but not to *Hamlet*, *King Lear*, or any of the great
reflective passages.

This would scarcely need saying were it not that
Goethe had it in him to touch these universal deeps of
poetry, and in due course did touch them.   He is,
perhaps, the only poet since Shakespeare of whom we can
say so much.   But he could not touch them by following
Shakespeare, he had to approach them in another way.
Those who hold that he could have made himself a
German Shakespeare if he had wished, that he could
have steered his genius into the Shakespearean ocean
and given us a succession of genuinely Shakespearean
masterpieces, must base their argument on the solitary
evidence of the first Adelheid, and they will find that
she is not enough to meet their need.

CHAPTER II

IT is an unexpected poem of Goethe's which couples Shakespeare and Charlotte von Stein as the two personalities that moulded him. "Lida [Charlotte], the joy of nearness; William, the distant star; what I am I owe to you":

> Lida! Glück der nächsten Nähe,
> William! Stern der höchsten Höhe,
> Euch verdank' ich was ich bin.

Was ever a human pair so oddly assorted—Shakespeare, the lawless poet; Charlotte, the lady at court: Shakespeare, the dramatic ideal; Charlotte, the loved in person: Shakespeare, the world-famous; Charlotte, remembered only for Goethe's sake? And, Charlotte apart, why this singling out of Shakespeare? Why not Herder, who taught him, incontestably, his first great lesson and continued to teach him until the pupil outgrew the master; Herder, who loosed his vital conception of literature upon him at the most susceptible moment of his life and flooded him with waves of poetry from every quarter? If we set Herder aside as being possibly less an influence than a transmitter of influences, it does not help much. In the throng of influences which played on Goethe in those teeming years there is no evident priority. Except for this one short poem there is nothing to tell us that Goethe owed more to Shakespeare than he owed to his beloved Strassburg Cathedral, or to the Greek of Homer and Pindar, which he studied and revelled deeply in. What we find is such a converging and overlapping of enthusiasms that it is impossible to sort them out. The rhapsody on Erwin von Steinbach seems indistinguishable from the rhapsody on Shakespeare.

But the poem is there, and what it says it says firmly and without haste. It is Shakespeare whom Goethe picks out of the melting-pot of the early seventies, and it is Charlotte, sole queen of the strange years that followed, who goes with him. "The days," he says, completing the poem, "are fled, but in those hours lies all my worth":

> Tag und Jahre sind verschwunden,
> Und doch ruht auf jenen Stunden
> Meines Wertes Vollgewinn;

thus intimately does he associate the two experiences, ignoring the gulf that lies between them. Yet time, if it lessened the gulf for Goethe, has not lessened it for us. To turn from *Götz von Berlichingen* or *Egmont* to either of the Charlotte dramas—to *Iphigenie auf Tauris* or *Torquato Tasso*, works conceived and established during the early years in Weimar when his spirit was in most intimate communion with hers—is probably as surprising in the twentieth century as it was in the eighteenth. True, we may overlook the difference and content ourselves with getting the best out of both worlds, and if we do this, reading *Iphigenie auf Tauris* and *Torquato Tasso*, when we come to them, for their own sakes and as works apart, we may find them among the most intelligible, as they are assuredly among the most lovable, of Goethe's poems. It is only when we try to relate them to the earlier Goethe or, for that matter, to the rest of Goethe that their perplexing character emerges. This, though it is true of both poems, is conspicuously true of *Iphigenie auf Tauris* which, taken alone, is easy reading but, taken as Goethe, is difficult and even problematical.

Iphigenie auf Tauris is a modernization of Euripides. Euripides, it will be remembered, tells of the adventurous mission of Orestes and Pylades to the land of the Taurians (Tauris, as Goethe calls it) to recover the

stolen image of Artemis (Goethe's Diana). Arriving
there, they find Iphigenia in exile, outwit the barbarian
king, their captor, with her connivance, and escape with
her and with the image. It is a typical combination
of courage and cunning, in which the quicker Greek
intelligence comes well to the fore. Goethe's trans-
formation of this tale is as sublime as it is skilful. For
the power of deceit he substitutes the power of truth.
Orestes, acting blindly on this new motive, confesses
his identity to the strange priestess into whose hands
he comes as a sacrificial victim. "I cannot endure," he
cries, "that thou shouldst be deceived with a lying word,
O noble soul. Let strangers set for strangers their
woven trap of lies with practised cunning. Between us
let there be truth. I am Orestes." This indiscretion
brings its reward. The priestess is Iphigenie, and
Orestes finds in her a sister and an ally. She in her turn
is unable to deceive King Thoas; instead, she confesses
the plot to him, puts their three lives in his hands, and
says: "Destroy us if you can find it in your heart to do
it." (Verdirb uns—wenn du darfst.) Thoas, after a
struggle, bows to the moral challenge and with a manly
sorrow bids them depart. The issue between Goethe
and Euripides is summed up in the conversation of
Orestes and Pylades in Act II. Pylades, the guiding
spirit of the adventure and the true Greek in Euripides'
sense, is all for strategy and refuses to admit that
cunning and intelligence disgrace the man of action, but
Orestes taunts him, saying: "You talk like Ulysses,"
and upholding the man who combines courage with
honesty. (Ich schätze den, der tapfer ist und grad.)

This moral simplicity is unlike Goethe, and it is
deceptive. The poem is not simple. The Greek gods
are its nominal deities, and there are passages in which
they seem to be its real deities. In the "Song of the
Fates," with its magnificent picture of the gods feasting
at golden tables, striding from mountain to mountain,

and hurling those whom they disfavour into the deep chasms below them, and again in the tales of the house of Tantalus, told by Iphigenie and Orestes, Goethe approaches that complete recapture of the Hellenic spirit which he finally achieved in his *Achilleis* and his *Helena*. Indeed, there are lines here and there in which we recover as much of the weight and the accent of Æschylus as we can expect in modern literature. The gods who come to life at these moments are they who fought with Titans, appointed the Furies, and took their toll of human sacrifice. But elsewhere we are in another and a far from Grecian world, in which Iphigenie prays to Diana in accents by no means alien to those which Gretchen uses before the image of the Virgin. "Thou hast clouds," she says, "O gracious goddess and saviour, in which to wrap the innocent that are persecuted":

> Du hast Wolken, gnädige Retterin,
> Einzuhüllen unschuldig Verfolgte.

She says that we "misunderstand the gods if we think them bloodthirsty," and she insists on her right to interpret the gods in her own way. When Thoas objects that "it is not the gods speaking, but her own heart," she replies that "it is only through our hearts that they speak to us."

This is a dilemma which Iphigenie never acknowledges. She is at variance with her gods, but she refuses to admit it. She holds that they are the same gods as those her fathers worshipped, the gods of feud and bloodshed, yet she also wishes to make them the sponsors of an opposite view, where all is gentleness and moral purity. When in her opening monologue she confesses her reluctance to serve Diana, we may recognize that she is speaking, dramatically, in reference to her exile and homesickness, but we cannot easily put aside the suspicion that she is also speaking, without knowing it, in terms of the discrepancy which lurks in her mind and in the poem. The lines say exactly what she might say if she were beginning to see herself as a modern reader sees her. Yet, discrepancy or not, it is essential to the poem that she should close her eyes to this issue—the issue between her faith and her dogma—and resolutely believe in the identity of the old gods with the new. This is a prop without which the work cannot stand; neither as poem nor as drama can it dispense with it.

It is easy to read the work without noticing the discrepancy, chiefly perhaps because Goethe manages to suggest—not explicitly, for the plot would not allow it—that the old order is changing, and that the old gods are changing with it. When Orestes hears the Furies go down to Tartarus and clang the brazen gates behind them with the noise of distant thunder, we feel that they will not return that way, and that his redemption has removed a mythological terror from the world, substituting a remediable agony of conscience for a wellnigh irremediable. And when Iphigenie fears lest she should find in her gentle heart the old pagan hatred stirring, we look down a vista of time from the beginnings of a humane order to the remote order from which it grew. It is a noble conception, this flowering of the modern world in the ancient, and Goethe's mastery of it is above question. From the opening lines, in which a Greek patriotism speaks with the voice of heart's desire, to the closing lines, in which a Germanic sense of allegiance blends with a Hellenic sense of hospitality, there is not a wrong or a hesitant note. The two worlds may be historically, they may be philosophically irreconcilable—in this poem they are beautifully reconciled. For sheer goodness of heart and Classical austerity combined—the simple thanksgiving of a child spoken with the dignity of Athenian drama—Sophocles and German pietism rolled in one—there is nothing comparable with Iphigenie's words of gratitude to the gods for sending her brother Orestes after these years of banishment. "As we know a king by the lavishness of his gifts—for that must seem little to him that is wealth to thousands —so we know you gods by bounties long withheld and wisely prepared. For you alone know what is good for us, and can see the spreading future when night by night the stars and the mist close our view. Calmly you hear our prayers that childishly implore you to hasten, but never do your hands pluck the golden fruits of heaven before they are ripe, and woe to him who impatiently snatches them, eats the bitter food, and dies":

> Wie man den König an dem Übermass
> Der Gaben kennt—denn ihm muss wenig scheinen,
> Was Tausenden schon Reichtum ist—so kennt
> Man euch, ihr Götter, an gesparten, lang'
> Und weise zubereiteten Geschenken.
> Denn ihr allein wisst, was uns frommen kann,
> Und schaut der Zukunft ausgedehntes Reich,
> Wenn jedes Abends Stern- und Nebelhülle
> Die Aussicht uns verdeckt. Gelassen hört
> Ihr unser Flehn, das um Beschleunigung
> Euch kindisch bittet; aber eure Hand
> Bricht unreif nie die goldnen Himmelsfrüchte,
> Und wehe dem, der, ungeduldig sie
> Ertrotzend, saure Speise sich zum Tode
> Geniesst.

The emotional unity is flawless. But the fallacy remains and it is the more to be reckoned with because it is uncharacteristic of Goethe. The older deities are in disgrace, yet the fact is not admitted, and they retain the shadow of office. The poem is, as it were, a twilight of the gods, in which we agree to pretend that their sun is still in mid-heaven, when their doom is already sealed. For the passionate truthfulness of Iphigenie and the dark confessional instincts of Orestes form a more powerful armament against Olympus than any battle-array of their Titan ancestors, and when the Scythian Thoas yields finally to the words of enlightenment which his priestess speaks to him, the old gods verily cease to exist. Yet they are with Iphigenie to the last, even in her words of parting.

Coming from Goethe this is peculiar. A few years earlier or a few years later—before Weimar or after Italy—it would have been impossible for his mind to work in this way. To be sure, in his earlier years in Strassburg and Frankfurt the gods had been frequently on his lips, but with how different an accent! It is one of the glories of his early poetic life, once it was truly quickened in him, that he was able to take great literature from any source and make its heroic figures his contemporaries in a world of springtime and ineffable promise. Herder, no doubt, helped him to this, but the finer statement of it is Goethe's. Here there is only one radiant world of consciousness, it is young and eternal, and all the gods and poets of all the ages have their being in it. We may look for this rapturous mood anywhere in Goethe between 1770 and 1775, but it is at its best in letters to Herder, and in the series of rhymeless odes centring about "Ganymed," in which the shining Greek myth of the youth borne heavenwards is shot through with modern yearning, and in which, as never before, the four words "Sacred Feeling, Infinite Beauty":

> Heilig Gefühl,
> Unendliche Schöne!

are fused in one surging emotion. "Ganymed," and its fellows—"An Schwager Kronos," "Wanderers Sturm-lied," and other pieces—owe everything to this delighted mingling of past and present, Classical, Germanic, Christian. Perhaps the clearest example of it is "Der Wandrer." Here, in a picture of a peasant household set down among the ruins of Roman architecture—with rocks, trees, and water round about—Classical and Hebrew, ancient and modern, nature and archæology, dwell together like one family. This is the period of

Goethe's life in which he is capable of exclaiming in a moment of exasperation, "God forgive the gods"— Gott verzeih's den Göttern die so mit uns spielen (letter to Kestner, 25th April, 1773)—a phrase which perhaps no other poet has used with this amusing ingenuousness, but which comes quite naturally from one who has pooled the mythologies and is living with them all on easy terms.

When Goethe conceived *Iphigenie auf Tauris* he was in Weimar, and this commingled rapture was over. And by the time he was putting the finishing touches to it he was in Rome and had travelled to the sharpest of differentiations. He was now in spirit—and he was soon to be in reality—the author of the *Roman Elegies*, in which for a while he parts company with the Christian era and the Northern world, and lives with Propertius and Ovid. How successfully let a quotation from the third Elegy show. "The arrows of love are various: some scratch the skin and the heart sickens for years with the creeping poison. But others, strongly winged and freshly sharpened, cut to the marrow and quickly fire the blood. In the heroic age when gods and goddesses loved, desire followed on seeing and fulfilment on desire. Do you think the Goddess of Love took long to reflect when she found Anchises pleasing in the grove of Ida? If Luna had tarried to kiss the fair sleeper, envious Aurora would quickly have wakened him. Hero saw Leander at the noisy feast, and straightway the lover plunged burning into the dark waters":

> Vielfach wirken die Pfeile des Amor: einige ritzen,
> Und vom schleichenden Gift kranket auf Jahre das Herz.
> Aber mächtig befiedert, mit frisch geschliffener Schärfe
> Dringen die andern ins Mark, zünden behende das Blut.
> In der heroischen Zeit, da Götter und Göttinnen liebten,
> Folgte Begierde dem Blick, folgte Genuss der Begier.
> Glaubst du, es habe sich lange die Göttin der Liebe besonnen,
> Als im Idäischen Hain einst ihr Anchises gefiel?

Hätte Luna gesäumt, den schönen Schläfer zu küssen,
O, so hätt' ihn geschwind, neidend, Aurora geweckt.
Hero erblickte Leandern am lauten Fest, und behende
Stürzte der Liebende sich heiss in die nächtliche Flut.

Goethe is no longer feeling his way towards the antique spirit. He has found it at last, as far as a modern poet can. His position now is as clear as it had been in Frankfurt; here it is wholly Classical, there it had been wholly indiscriminate. Midway between these unequivocal extremes comes the strangely equivocal *Iphigenie auf Tauris*, with its subtle misappropriation of the Greek mythology, its exotic humanitarianism, and its orthodoxy. Not that it is orthodox in any dogmatic sense, but it is orthodox in its psychology, in the analysis of life on which it is based. There was nothing of this in the earlier period; its ecstatic naturalism is as foreign to our orthodoxy as the studied naturalism of the years after Italy. But here in *Iphigenie auf Tauris* it is different; here, if we look below the deceptive surface, we find the familiar dualism, the soul-and-body psychology of the Christian era. Nor is it always below the surface. When Iphigenie says in the most famous of her lines that she is "seeking the land of the Greeks with her soul":

Das Land der Griechen mit der Seele suchend,

she is voicing this dualism in the clearest terms, and she is sounding the dominant note of a poem in which from first to last the emphasis is on the soul rather than on the Greeks. It is the soul and the moral order which the soul requires that are the presiding agencies of the poem, and Apollo, Diana, the Furies, and what not, have to conform to their mandates. And seeing that Iphigenie is neither a goddess nor a law to herself—there is scarcely a breath of revolt or self-assertion in the poem—we have to shift the authority, as Iphigenie would have shifted it, from her individual soul to that

supreme sphere which her soul knows and obeys, but
for which there is no real habitat in the poem. By
ignoring the fact that the foundations of the old celestial
machinery are undermined Goethe avoids the problem
of reconstructing it, and excludes from the outward
substance of the poem what is most vital in our analysis
of it—the moral order enthroned above it.

Nothing could be farther from his usual practice.
He never attempted the like again, and we may doubt
whether he could have carried it off in this case, if the
poem had not been spiritually completed in his first
draft of it. If, instead of facing the purely stylistic
problem of converting iambic prose into blank verse,
he had been called upon, as he usually was, to develop
or to re-cast his poem, it is unlikely that he would have
been able to sustain it in its peculiar compromise. He
would have stumbled on the vacuum in it, and started
again. How near he was to doing so is well shown by a
phrase which crept in at the last. "These many years,"
says Iphigenie in the final version of the poem, "I have
been kept here by some high will to which I submit."
(Ein hoher Wille, dem ich mich ergebe.) Here, and
nowhere else, Goethe gives a name to that higher seat
of authority which both the character of Iphigenie and
the prevailing accents of the poem call for and hints
directly at the otherworldliness, the transcendentalism
in his work which he cannot bring himself to acknowledge. And while we may be glad that he succeeded in
this evasion, because without it we should not possess
Iphigenie auf Tauris as it is, we have to recognize the
attendant limitations of the poem — the something
suppressed, the something arrested in its inner life,
which sets it in curious contrast with the rest of Goethe.
For we find in the end that we cannot take its spiritual
logic an inch farther than he takes it. Gravely moral
as the poem is, it does not feed our moral life as it should,
coming from him. Much as we admire it and return

to it, we see it as a special case, memorable always, but somehow fruitless. And we see it to least advantage as a treatment of the problem of truth and truth-telling, if we come to it from Molière or Ibsen, from *Le Misanthrope* or *The Wild Duck*.

Thus powerfully did the conventional mind of Charlotte sway the poet's genius. When we turn to *Torquato Tasso*, which she also inspired, we can see the same dominant spell at work, curbing, refining, spiritualizing. Like *Iphigenie auf Tauris* the poem is suffused with a transcendentalism which it does not stress. But the case is different. In *Iphigenie auf Tauris* the case was obscured by the subject. Or rather the subject lent itself to the obscuring which we suspect Goethe instinctively desired; it enabled him to express his state of mind without voicing it directly, without facing it, without committing himself to it. In *Torquato Tasso* he makes the same evasion, but by an opposite device of the poetic instinct. He chooses as his central figure one of the most transcendental of poets, and then studies him untranscendentally in an episode of his practical life. Once more Goethe succeeds in liberating his mood without admitting to it. If in *Iphigenie auf Tauris* he took a transcendental theme to a practical world, he now reverses the procedure and takes a practical theme to a transcendental world. In each case the transcendentalism is kept down; it is felt rather than stated, subconscious and pervasive rather than explicitly recognized.

Of the two *Torquato Tasso*, the later choice, is also the happier, because it avoids the confining fallacy which lurks in *Iphigenie auf Tauris*. The subject is never at variance with the poet's thought, and this in the end makes it the richer poem. While *Iphigenie auf Tauris* moves perplexingly from Hellas to the Augustan Age, from the *Eumenides* of Æschylus to Lessing's *Nathan the Wise*, *Torquato Tasso* preserves a happy mean in the

Renaissance Platonism echoed with admirable simplicity
in its opening scene. "It is not we he loves," says one
Leonore to the other, "he takes what he loves from every
sphere, and calls it by the name that is our name. He
imparts his feeling to us. We think we love him, but
we only unite with him in loving the highest that it is
in us to love":

> Uns liebt er nicht—verzeih, dass ich es sage!—
> Aus allen Sphären trägt er, was er liebt,
> Auf einen Namen nieder, den wir führen,
> Und sein Gefühl teilt er uns mit; wir scheinen
> Den Mann zu lieben, und wir lieben nur
> Mit ihm das Höchste, was wir lieben können.

In this essential idealism, and in the talk of the Golden
Age which soon follows, we can hear the keynote of this
aristocratic poem. "The Golden Age, ah, whither is it
flown?" cries Tasso to the Princess, and he hastens to
recall the time "when an ancient tree in a bright meadow
gave shade to shepherd and shepherdess, while lesser
bushes enclosed the yearning lovers with their tender
twigs":

> Da ein uralter Baum auf bunter Wiese
> Dem Hirten und der Hirtin Schatten gab,
> Ein jüngeres Gebüsch die zarten Zweige
> Um sehnsuchtsvolle Liebe traulich schlang.

If the Princess replies that there never was a Golden
Age save in the sense in which there still is one, she does
nothing to destroy it, she merely shifts it farther into
the inner life and establishes it more securely in her
secret heart and in the heart of the poem.

We learn to look for nature in Goethe's poetry, but
there is little of it here, and that little is vague
and artificial, like the Golden Age itself. The trees are
there for Tasso to pin his verses to, and that is all we
know about them. After they have served this purpose
they can be forgotten. When the poem opens it is
springtime, but we do not see nature bursting into
joyous life as in the Strassburg lyrics, or serenely blooming

as in the sunny uplands which grace the later pages of
Faust. All we see is the gardener quietly removing the
winter covering from the domesticated citron-trees, and
the flowers looking at us with children's eyes from their
nursery flower-beds. It is a strictly interior study.
When the Princess says that for her "the splendour of
the sun, the joy of the high noon, and the rich variety
of the outer world is barren and wrapt in mist," she is
speaking for the poem as much as for herself. And
there is a similar appropriateness when Tasso, like Faust
of the woodland cavern, seeks or imagines himself
seeking the solitude of nature, only to encounter—as
Faust did not—a sudden vision of Elysium which wipes
all thought of nature from his mind and transports him
from Mother Earth to some Pantheon of the Golden
Age, where he joins the heroes of old. Here, as everywhere in this poem, the light of nature fades out against
the stronger light of the spirit. In the one memorable
nature passage in *Torquato Tasso* it is death, not life,
which is contemplated, and of all natural deaths the most
withdrawn and mystical—the death of the silkworm
which spins itself away and finds a new life. It is St.
Teresa's metaphor, the perfect metaphor of the trans-
cendentalist. "Forbid the silkworm to spin," cries
Tasso, "when it is spinning itself to death. It unwinds
the precious web from within, and never ceases till it
has enclosed itself in its coffin. Would that the fate of
this enviable worm might be ours, swiftly to unfold our
joyous wings in a new vale of sunlight":

> Verbiete du dem Seidenwurm, zu spinnen,
> Wenn er sich schon dem Tode näher spinnt:
> Das köstliche Geweb' entwickelt er
> Aus seinem Innersten, und lässt nicht ab,
> Bis er in seinen Sarg sich eingeschlossen.
> O geb' ein guter Gott uns auch dereinst
> Das Schicksal des beneidenswerten Wurms,
> Im neuen Sonnental die Flügel rasch
> Und freudig zu entfalten.

It is just the same in *Iphigenie auf Tauris*. Nature
has no part in it, and its absence is the more noticeable
because the theme, as it comes to Goethe's hand, is so
rich in nature. For the choruses of Euripides, racy
with the salt-sea air and the prowess of heroes, we
have the prayers and introspections of Orestes and his
sister. In this modern poem there is scarcely an open
door for the sea-breeze to enter; it is even more closeted
than *Torquato Tasso*, where, at least, we are free to pace
the garden-paths and watch the snow melt on the distant
mountains. There is only one moment at which the
play of nature-forces breaks in notably upon the life of
the spirit. It is in the healing of Orestes, but even
here the thunderstorm which symbolizes the healing is
enacted in Orestes' mind only and does not fill and
enlarge the poem.

So close are these two plays to the spirit of Charlotte
that if we know them well we know all Goethe's relation
to her. The love-poems and the letters express the
relation more directly, but they alter nothing, they
simply corroborate. Consider the first, and most
instructive, of his poems to her, dated 14th April, 1776,
and beginning: "Warum gabst du uns die tiefen Blicke."
In this poem Goethe asks why they twain should be
different from other lovers who live in enviable blindness,
scarcely knowing their own hearts—taking their joy
and their pain unquestioningly as it comes—while he
and she, foredoomed to a fatal clear-sightedness, cannot
surrender themselves to illusions, as others do, and
snatch the fruits of bliss. On the face of it, this seems
to be the confession of a thwarted intercourse such as
might readily develop between one man and the wife of
another. But this is not the real, certainly not the
whole meaning of the words. What Goethe seems to
say, in lines which are as elusive as they are eternally
fascinating, is that the key to their imperfect happiness
lies not in their being thwarted—though this may

D

accord with the outer facts which we know, but which are not a constituent part of the poem—but in their being too close. They have more than other lovers, they can read each other as they read themselves, and they pay the price for it. Their knowledge is bought at the price of illusion, and without illusion there is no delight.

And now in his despair at a union made tragic by its completeness he asks whether in some remote past she must not have been his wife or his sister, living with him in an ideal intercourse which lingers dream-like in the memory and torments them in their present dilemma. Again we may remind ourselves of the social barrier between them, and again the poem takes us deeper and bids us witness the present state of lovers—in a world which compels them to choose between a transient happiness and the pain of fuller knowledge—and contrast it with the heavenly bliss of lovers in another world where rapture feeds on truth and truth on rapture. "And of all this only a memory lingers in the uncertain heart. It feels the old truth unchanged within, and the new condition pains it. We seem but half in life, the bright day is dark around us ":

> Und von allem dem schwebt ein Erinnern
> Nur noch um das ungewisse Herz,
> Fühlt die alte Wahrheit ewig gleich im Innern,
> Und der neue Zustand wird ihm Schmerz.
> Und wir scheinen uns nur halb beseelet,
> Dämmernd ist um uns der hellste Tag.

This poem, like others of Goethe's best, is as difficult spiritually as it is verbally lucid. But it is clearly transcendental in issue, because it reproduces the movement of his thought and feeling from an immediate world which has become intolerable to a dream-world which he has no choice but to create. We see the desire for illusion—utterly foreign to him at other times—taking control of him in this new crisis, forcing its dream of happiness and perfection upon him, and tincturing his creative mind with the poetry of escape. We see him entering the Golden Age that other poets have entered, but entering it reluctantly, as an exile. It is as if this poem recorded the precise moment of his life at which he qualified for the authorship of *Iphigenie auf Tauris* and *Torquato Tasso*.

There seems to be no point at which the poems and the letters to Charlotte fail to tally with the plays. This first poem to her is unusual in modern love-poetry in that it speaks for two and not for one. Goethe is not just singing his feelings, he is involving his beloved in every word he utters, making the poem—as he believes —as much hers as his, so that it is not centred in his heart alone, but in their twin hearts, their relationship. That is why the poem can claim, as it does, that the uniqueness of the love it commemorates lies in the excessive closeness, even the identity, of the lovers. For Goethe this was a novel experience, never repeated. He had not written thus of Friederike or Lili, nor was he to write thus of Christiane or Ulrike. The tragic emotion of his love for Ulrike is strictly his private emotion and springs precisely from his sense of difference. Ulrike teaches him the greatest of lessons, but it is wasted on him, he cannot profit by it. "What good," he cries, "is this high wisdom to me?" The lines to Charlotte close on the opposite note of comradeship and an inseparable fate. He is "happy that the destiny which torments them cannot change them":

> Glücklich, dass das Schicksal, das uns quälet,
> Uns doch nicht verändern mag!

This distinctive aspect of Goethe's love for Charlotte is duly repeated in *Iphigenie auf Tauris* and *Torquato Tasso* which, unlike the rest of Goethe's highest poetical work, deal with personal relationships rather than with individual or philosophical problems. Tasso's dilemma is different from Werther's or Faust's in that it is wholly induced by others. His business, he is given to understand, is to consolidate a successful friendship with Antonio, the man of affairs. He does his best, and it brings him to the brink of tragedy. That is the essence of the plot. Tasso is not, like Werther, busied with an inner problem, though we feel that he is capable of being so busied; he is not in serious doubt, as Faust is, how his life should be spent; he does not despair of his artistic gifts or of his soul's salvation. The immediate cause of his despair is, in a restricted sense, social. If the world would leave him alone all would be well, or, to put it more accurately, all would be different, the problem would be changed. But the world refuses to leave him alone, and prefers to torture him on the rack of its conventions.

Something may be due here to Goethe's problem of adjustment to court life at Weimar after the bourgeois freedom of his native city, but it is difficult to see how this problem, a trivial one at most, could ever have assumed in his mind the tragic intensity necessary for the creation of *Torquato Tasso*. Surely the deeper reason for this tragedy of relationships lay in his closeness to Charlotte von Stein, which, dominating his poetic consciousness, made the individualism of *Faust* or *Werther* for the time being impossible. It is significant that not a line of *Faust* is known to have been written in the years between Frankfurt and Italy, and that the Faustian note is scarcely sounded in the poetry of the period.

Moreover we find in *Iphigenie auf Tauris*, which is socially more remote from Weimar, the same preoccupation with relationships as in *Torquato Tasso*. To be sure, it is not here a matter of the social proprieties, as it partly is in *Torquato Tasso*, unless we argue that the sense of moral obligation which Iphigenie awakens in Orestes and which she in her turn feels towards Thoas represents the social proprieties at an unspoiled and elementary stage. But the poem turns not less surely than *Torquato Tasso* upon relationships. Even the madness and healing of Orestes, tinged as it is with individualism and the Werther mood, is no exception, because Orestes owes his recovery to the presence of his sister and the moral regeneration which she inspires; in short, he owes it to another. The rest is entirely a matter of adjustments between individuals; Iphigenie, Thoas, Pylades have no dilemmas beyond those which arise out of their being thrown together.

The letters in their turn are all of a piece with the verses. Charlotte, they tell us, is Goethe's inseparable companion and his unattainable Madonna, his ideal and his *alter ego*. "You seem to me of late," he writes, "like the Madonna going up to heaven. In vain does one that is left below stretch out his arms to her, in vain does his tearful parting gaze desire hers again, she is lost in the splendour that surrounds her, yearning only for the crown that hovers over her head." And, at a later date: "My soul is grown into yours. I have no use for words, you know that I am inseparable from you, and that neither high nor low can divide me from you." This is just what Tasso says to the Princess, distilling the everyday poetry of the letters into maturer verse. "An ineffable power flows from your lips, mastering me. Yes, you make me wholly yours. Nothing of my whole self is mine henceforth":

> Unsägliche Gewalt, die mich beherrscht,
> Entfliesset deinen Lippen; ja, du machst
> Mich ganz dir eigen. Nichts gehöret mehr
> Von meinem ganzen Ich mir künftig an.

It is still a far cry from Charlotte to Shakespeare, but the case for associating them is now clear—Charlotte, not less than Shakespeare, stood to Goethe for a kind of poetry, and induced, or partially induced, a kind of poetry in him. Owing, we must assume, to something compulsive in her, but owing still more to some extra-ordinary faculty of adaptation in Goethe, the poetry which he wrote under her influence is as easily distin-guishable in texture from the rest of him as his Shake-spearean poetry. There is nothing quite like it else-where. What normally happens when a poet is inspired by a woman is that he writes in accordance with his own temperament, not with hers. She may fertilize him with poetry, but the offspring is his, and takes his character. It is only in this one anomalous instance that the mistress of a poet's heart is also the mistress of his poetry, imposing her discipline on it as surely as if she were another author and he were imitating her. And in this sense Goethe could look upon her in later life exactly as he looked upon Shakespeare, not as one he had known or loved, but as a poet and a teacher. Thus there is no incongruity in his pairing of Lida with William, and there is no paradox.

But is there no paradox in his contention that these two were the making of him? That they shared in the making of him is obvious, since between them they dominated no inconsiderable portion of his early life, but it is not less obvious that they might have shared in his unmaking, because they enticed him—first Shakespeare and then Charlotte—into ways of poetry that would have been detrimental, if not fatal, to him in the long run. He was a poet who could only count on writing at his best when he wrote in the lyrical way about himself and his experiences, and in Shakespeare he found a master of the dramatic way, a master who incited him to blow the breath of life into characters and situations which he had never experienced and could only know in imagination. He was also a poet so dependent on nature that without nature, without the thoughts and feelings which nature communicated, poetry would have died in him, and in Charlotte he found a way of poetry which was frankly antagonistic

to nature, and held itself responsible only to the soul
and to the inner life. Neither way—neither the imaginative way of Shakespeare nor the spiritual way of Charlotte—would have sufficed him permanently, and it was
a right instinct which made him drift away from the
one and break outright with the other. To this extent
Goethe's lines on Lida and William are misleading, and
the works they inspired in him unrepresentative.

CHAPTER III

BY the time Goethe was clear of these two influences he was no longer a youthful poet. When he made the journey to Italy which gave him back to himself and enabled him to move in directions of his own choosing, he was approaching forty and had taken surprisingly long to reach this freedom. But, after all, freedom was not new to him. He had felt his freedom long before and had written strictly in his own right while still a beginner. The proof of this lies in a variety of early pieces, but notably in two longer productions— *Werther*, a novel in letters, and the *Urfaust*, the first stage of *Faust*.

If these two works are not always mentioned together it is not surprising. As it happened, *Werther* was published immediately and shared the immense popularity of *Götz von Berlichingen*, while the *Urfaust* was quietly put aside, to be resumed later. It is only in recent times that a manuscript copy has come to light and established the *Urfaust* as a distinctive work of Goethe's. To the world at large the Goethe who went to Weimar in 1775 was the author of *Werther* and *Götz von Berlichingen*, and the rest of him was unknown or subsidiary. Coming as these two works did in fairly quick succession and just when the time was ripe, they have been closely associated from the start, and the most has been made of their similarity—their informal style, their love of the simple life, their joint protest against the conventions. Yet the difference, the psychological difference, is startling, as we can see from Werther's reaction to the pictorial mood so joyfully

evidenced in *Götz von Berlichingen*.   If in the writing of
this play Goethe delighted in the colour and the panorama of life, in *Werther* he turns from it with a tragic
revulsion.   And the old peep-show comparison, never
far from Goethe's mind in these early years, is there to
point the transition.   "What is life without love?"
asks Werther in an early letter; "it is a magic-lantern
without light.   As soon as you bring in the lamp you
see the gayest of pictures on your white screen.   And
even if they are nothing but passing phantoms, they
can be a joy to us when we stand in front of them like
happy boys and revel in the wondrous shows."   Here,
though the mood is comparatively serene, the clouds are
gathering.   Werther, we feel, has lost his first delight
in the world of appearance, and the comfort it gives him
is precarious.   The sense of transience is already hanging
over him, and before long it dominates him.   "If you
could see me," he writes a little later, "in the throng of
distractions, how stagnant I am.   Never for a moment
does my heart overflow, never an hour's real happiness.
Nothing!   Nothing!   I seem to stand before a raree-
show (Raritätenkasten) and see people and horses
jerked this way and that, and often I ask myself if it
is not an optical illusion.   I play my part too, or rather
I have to play it, like a marionette, and many a time I
seize my neighbour by his wooden hand and shrink back
in horror."   This passage occurs early in the second
book, under the date of 30th January, after Werther
has obtained his remove and exchanged the dear com-
panionship of Lotte and Albert for the conventional
life at the embassy.   He is at the point of closest and
most unwelcome contact with the practical world, and
he uses the raree-show—symbol of Goethe's youthful
delight in Shakespeare little more than two years before
—to express his disgust at it.

These passages serve to remind us how unpictorial is
the art of *Werther* as compared with its less reflective

predecessor. In *Götz von Berlichingen* all seems visually circumscribed—unless we except the Adelheid adventure which broke its bounds in the first draft—each scene-picture being as clearly contained and filled as if it were a painter's canvas framed in its rectangle. *Werther*, on the other hand, has no statable dimensions and is perpetually out of focus. "Dämmernd" is Werther's word for this, and he is never weary of using it.

The gradual loosening of Werther's hold on the phenomenal world is finely illustrated by the shifting of his interest from Homer to Ossian. Homer—perhaps the clearest in profile of great poets—is at first his sole companion. Sitting in summer-time by the well, Werther watches the girls who come from the town to fetch water—"the most harmless," he says, "and the most necessary of occupations which aforetime was done by the kings' daughters"—and in this patriarchal spirit, half Old Testament and half Odyssey, he solaces himself with his beloved Homer. His birthday present—on the twenty-eighth of August, Goethe's birthday—is the little Wetstein Homer—"two little volumes in duodecimo"—which he has long desired in place of the heavy Ernesti edition. And a little before this date he writes: "You ask if you are to send me my books. My dear fellow, I pray you for God's sake, spare me them. I do not wish to be guided, encouraged, stimulated. This heart of mine is turbulent enough. What I need is a lullaby, and I find plenty of this in my Homer."

The reader of Homer who can extract a lullaby from him is reading him strangely, and is in danger of deserting him. When this finally happens—"Ossian has supplanted Homer in my affections," he writes after an interval—we realize that it had to come. Werther is enraptured now with the grey mists and the moonlight of Ossian's shadowy world. And it is Ossian, the vague and featureless, who is with him to the end.

This is the instinctive movement of his mind, traceable even in his happiest moments. When he sees the spring blossom—this is from the earliest of the letters—he exclaims that "every tree and every hedge is a nosegay," and that he "would fain become a mayfly to float in the sea of odour and find his nourishment there"—a typical impulse which closes up the outer world and substitutes a fervent, unvisual activity for the shrewder activity of seeing and watching. Werther is not observant of the natural beauty about him, he must shut his eyes and drift hither and thither in it like the mayfly. Whatever is specific or formal, be it in thought or act, he puts from him with an uncanny thoroughness. The decent logic of his friend Albert incenses him. "You know," he writes, "that I like him well, except for his 'but' (bis auf seine Zwar), for does it not go without saying that every general statement admits of exceptions? The fellow is so precise. If he thinks he has said anything hasty, general, or half true he is never done with his qualifying, modifying, adding, and subtracting, until there is nothing left." So intense, so absolute is his passion for the illimitable, that he prefers what men call inactivity to any tangible occupation. "I could not draw now, not a line, and I was never a greater painter than at these moments."

Having forfeited all sure hold upon the outer world, Werther will brook none within. He will have no mentor but his own heart, and it is without a tether. In this chosen world of intimations and vague desires he is like one lost in a spaceless sea. With growing alarm we watch the fluctuations of his mind from the near to the far, from the minute to the unbounded. More even than by the vehemence of his emotions, which makes Lotte fear that his excessive sympathy with everything will be his death, we are dismayed by his incalculable oscillations from high to low, from rapture to despair. It is with an imminent sense of catastrophe that we hear him exclaim at one moment that the might and splendour of the world will destroy him, and at another that there is no end to all this misery but the grave, or that Nature, once a nurturing mother and a paradise, is suddenly become "an engulfing and ruminating monster" (ein ewig verschlingendes, ewig wiederkäuendes Ungeheuer).

Werther's suicide is merely the outcome of this extreme way of living. He relinquishes or loses all contact with the outside world, all formal control of the mind within, all discipline of occupation and routine. His spirit arrogates to itself the freedom of the universe, and in due course the body follows and we lose sight of him for ever.

Werther can still be read with absorption. It is as near to our humanity now and as exciting as when it was first written, and it is likely to remain so. What we experience is not so much a suicide as the elimination of a personality, but the process is one that we could not have foreseen. Our individual profiles, this book tells us, must be preserved by usage, or they will disappear. For most of us the daily round and common task—the superficial concern with ourselves, with our particular wants and pleasures, the mere outward activity of our lives—preserves our outlines, our visible exteriors, until the physical processes are undermined by disease or decay, and we die. Until then the boundary line which hedges us off from the universe is trodden daily and hourly, and the pathway is clearly marked. But Werther is so incessantly, so passionately occupied with the essential, universal, absolute life which he finds deep down in himself and in things, that he neglects his personal boundaries, fails to tread the pathway, or to repair the fences which delimit his personal estate and mark him off from the vasty deep, and in due course he pays the price of this incaution and disappears beyond recall. To read his story is like watching an artist's study of a head, which by virtue of some unique and consuming vitality erases itself mysteriously before our eyes and leaves us staring at the blank sheet.

This is the real meaning of Werther's story. Unlike the suicide of Brutus or Anna Karenin, or any other in literature, it is essentially unmotived, and takes us rather to metaphysical poetry than to drama or prose fiction. Its counterpart in Goethe's works is the assumption of Ganymede in a burst of springtide exaltation or the all-but-suicide of Faust, who at the crucial moment forgets his impulse of despair at a supernal rebuff and sees only the limitless vista that awaits him beyond the narrow door; the difference being that these two are the responsible agents of the deed while Werther is the victim of it. His death is the inevitable consequence of his habit of life, not a separate act of will. It might have come earlier or later, the song of the angels which Faust heard might have deferred it or hastened it, but could never have averted it.

It is true that in another light the suicide can be ascribed to hopeless love, a thwarted career, and a case of pistols, and that Napoleon, for whom seven readings of *Werther* were apparently not enough, censured the mixing of the motives and, if we can trust the accounts of their somewhat disingenuous conversation, extracted from Goethe his concurrence in this censure. But the fact is, and Goethe must have known it, that in the deeper life of the work there was no need of specific motives; the suicide of Werther was not dependent on his meeting Lotte or on public disappointments or access to fire-arms. Give Werther his way of inner life, and a private paradise will not prevent his vanishing. For such a state of mind as his anything and everything is a motive for the last release.

There is nothing in the text of *Werther* to indicate that Goethe was closely interested in the external motives of the catastrophe, or was even careful of them.

We know that when he revised his text for a later edition he modified his conception of Albert, but the story had nothing to gain by the change, and it had something to lose, since by removing a certain invidiousness from Albert's character he made Werther's relations with him and Lotte less exasperating than before and thus tended to weaken the central situation. If Goethe had been primarily concerned with the dramatic psychology of his three characters, conceived as a group, he might have been reluctant to tamper with the text at this point. He seems instead merely to have accepted the Wetzlar material—chiefly his own intimate relation with Kestner and Lotte—as a suitable basis or stiffening for his theme, and to have devoted his main attention to the mind of Werther.

Not that he was unmindful of narrative technique, as his use of Homer and Ossian shows. If Goethe has a place among the masters of prose fiction it is as much on the strength of *Werther* as of any other work. But his skill as a story-teller shows up better in his management of the invented episodes than in his use of autobiography. Prominent among these is the episode—added later when the text was revised—of the love-lorn peasant lad who murders his supposed rival in an onset of jealousy, an episode which we instinctively connect with that of the idiot youth whose year of confinement in the madhouse is remembered by him as his lost happiness. These are the two figures in the story who bear most directly on Werther and best explain his mind to us. In one sense—the sense in which everything that happens to Werther is a motive for his final resolve—they thrust him on to his doom. He is aghast at a world in which the worthiest love can culminate in crime and murder, and he is not less aghast at the dreadful case of one whose happiness is indistinguishable from his insanity. "God in heaven, hast Thou decreed that men should only know happiness before they

come to their understanding, and when they lose it
again?"

But these figures serve chiefly for contrast. In Goethe's
eyes Werther is neither a criminal nor a lunatic. Or if
he is a criminal he is only technically so. The Law or
the Church may hold him guilty, but our common
humanity repudiates the charge. Werther is buried
without funeral rites, but simple workfolk carry him to
the grave. And if he is insane it is with the insanity
of genius, not of disease, the insanity of those who see
too deeply and pay the tragic penalty. "I have been
beyond myself more than once," says Werther, anticipating a famous passage in *Faust*, "my passions were
never far from madness, but I do not regret it. For I
have come to see in my fashion that extraordinary men
who do something great and seemingly impossible have
always been called fanatical and insane."

We have only to listen closely to Werther to hear a
clear mind speaking. If there must be a pathological
view of him there is also a normal one. Werther is
remote from conventional life and he abhors it, but he is
close to the man of genius, to the child, to nature.
His suicide is not so much an offence against nature as
an exemplification of that law of nature which says that
if we venture too far and too frequently from the shores
of the finite into the deeps of infinity we shall sooner or
later be caught by the deeps and never return. This is
a law which Nature is seldom called upon to enforce.
Werther alone, it may be, has succeeded in provoking
her to the enforcement, but the law remains and is not
less valid for being seldom broken. For Werther the
outer world of particular things and particular horizons
which calls the rest of us into action and gives us our
so-called liberty, is irksome and imprisoning. He can
only endure it so long as it lets him sense the eternal
life behind it, and it often fails him in his need. But
the door, the ever-open door, to this eternity is in the

depths of the heart. Here, where others are cabined
and confined, he is as free as a bird, and here he takes
his long flight at the last.

In his dissatisfaction with outward and visible things
Werther is at one with Tasso. For all the difference in
setting there is no mistaking the bond of sensibility
between them, the common shrinking from affairs which
has made each go into himself and cultivate another
way of living. Clearly, the traditional view which sees
Tasso as "Werther intensified" (ein gesteigerter Werther)
has something to support it. Nevertheless it is misleading. For one thing, Werther is at the breaking-point
continually, it is impossible to go farther in his direction
than he goes, an intenser Werther is scarcely con-
ceivable. Is it because *Werther* was written first that
it once seemed lower in pitch than *Torquato Tasso*?
Or because it was written in prose at a time when the
poetic power of prose was less readily conceded than it is
to-day? The most we can admit is that, if they must be
compared, the honours are even. But is comparison
possible? Can Werther's inwardness be measured
against Tasso's? Does their common need to withdraw
lead them to seek a common refuge? The refuge which
Werther seeks knows no locality. His desire is to
merge himself in the life that is everywhere in him and
about him, the life that he discovers whenever he
penetrates the surface of things and delves beneath—the
life of nature. Its centre is everywhere, it is in his heart
and it is in the heart of things. It shifts like the mayfly
which flits from bloom to bloom in a sea of odour, or
like the mists which roll, no matter where, in the shoreless
skies of Ossian. Tasso's dream-world is not thus omni-
present. It may borrow the trappings of nature for its
pastorals, but its centre is remote from the immediate
world; it is in the past, in memory, in the soul of man.
Tasso's elysium is a dream-picture in the placid waters
of the brook; forgetting nature for the moment, he sees

his vision. Werther's impulse is more metaphysical; he wishes to break through the limits of space, and be everywhere in nature at once. He is not content to experience what Goethe experienced at Ilmenau, when Nature promised him that her sleep would in due course be his, saying to him: "Wait, soon thou too shalt rest":

> Warte nur, balde
> Ruhest du auch.

He finds waiting intolerable. The tranquillity which Wordsworth knew when he remembered

> a sense sublime
> Of something far more deeply interfused,
> Whose dwelling is the light of setting suns,
> And the round ocean and the living air,
> And the blue sky, and in the mind of man,

is no tranquillity to him. It is not enough that he should have had his revelation, he wants it always and everywhere; he cannot learn. It is all said with moving simplicity in a paragraph.

"It is marvellous. When I came here and looked down the lovely valley from the hill, everything drew me to it. The coppice there—Oh, that I could mingle in its shadows! The hill-top yonder—Oh, to survey the wide domain from there! The chains of hills and the intimate valleys—if only I could lose myself in them! I hastened there, and returned, and had not found what I hoped. Oh, it is with distance as with the future. A darkling immensity (ein grosses dämmerndes Ganze) confronts us, our feelings and sight are blurred and lost in it, and we long to surrender ourselves, we long to be filled with the rapture of a single great emotion. And alas, when we go there and the Yonder becomes the Here, everything is as it was before. There we stand in our poverty and our limitation, and the soul pants for the refreshment that has escaped it."

This is just what Faust says when he contemplates

E

the sign of the Macrocosm in his book of magic. "What a spectacle, but alas, only a spectacle! Infinite Nature, where shall I reach thee, where shall I reach thy breasts, those sources of life that heaven and earth depend on and the famished heart yearns for? They give to drink, and shall I thus vainly languish?"

> Welch Schauspiel! aber ach ein Schauspiel nur!
> Wo fass ich dich, unendliche Natur?
> Euch Brüste wo? Ihr Quellen alles Lebens,
> An denen Himmel und Erde hängt,
> Dahin die welcke Brust sich drängt.
> Ihr quellt, ihr tränckt, und schmacht ich so vergebens?

And when he sees the sign of the Earth-Spirit it is Werther's impulse again. "My whole heart goes out to thee; yield, yield to me, though it should prove my death":

> Ich fühle ganz mein Herz dir hingegeben!
> Du musst! Du musst! Und kostet es mein Leben.

These brief extracts from the great opening scene of the *Urfaust* are all that is needed to show how close it is to *Werther*. It is not, as between the two individuals, Tasso and Werther, a temperamental affinity which weakens on inspection; it is a philosophical affinity, able to stand up under any scrutiny. The only difference apart from the difference in the fable—Werther is a melancholy eighteenth - century advocate, Faust the desperate alchemist of an older day—is that Faust has the driving force, the personal energy which Werther confesses he has lost. Werther seeks with self-abandonment what Faust seeks with proudest self-assertion. But for this—it is an important difference in the mettle of the two works—we should be tempted to call *Werther* a prose *Faust*, or *Faust* a metrical *Werther*. The melody which Faust sings is simply Werther's melody transposed into the major key.

In the *Urfaust* the philosophical impulses are all

stated by Faust in the opening scene. Of the two it is
Werther who explores the field more elaborately; Faust
at this stage simply vents his thought in one superb
outburst, and then leaves us in the dark as to what
follows. Yet if the *Urfaust* had stopped here at the
encounter with the Earth-Spirit it would be momentous.
In this passage of less than two hundred lines there is a
range of expression not attained by *Werther* or *Götz von
Berlichingen*, or any of the odes and lyrics of these years.
Almost every mood that we associate with Goethe's
youth is echoed in it. There is all the melting tenderness
of *Werther* in Faust's wish that the full moon "might
look for the last time on his anguish":

> O sähst du, voller Mondenschein,
> Zum lezten mal auf meine Pein.

There is the medieval colour of *Götz von Berlichingen* in
the high vaulting and the stained glass, "where even the
dear light of heaven breaks dimly through the painted
panes":

> Wo selbst das liebe Himmels Licht
> Trüb durch gemahlte Scheiben bricht.

There is the swelling note of *Prometheus*: "Am I a god?"

> Bin ich ein Gott? Mir wird so licht!

and the pungent irony of the early satires: "They call me
doctor and professor too, and these ten years now I have
led my pupils by the nose":

> Heisse Docktor und Professor gar,
> Und ziehe schon an die zehen Jahr
> Herauf herab und queer und krumm
> Meine Schüler an der Nas herum.

In this piece of wildly spontaneous writing Goethe
seems to pour out the whole of himself mood after mood,
and he changes from one mood to another with astonishing ease. Something has liberated him and given
him a new freedom of expression. It is not the philosophy of the passage, since *Werther* has all its philosophy

without commanding its vast emotional register. Nor is it the dramatic character of the legend, for the passage is pre-eminently lyrical and lyrically oblivious of plot or fable. The evidence points to something much simpler. The only other early works of Goethe's in which we find this flexibility and this range of feeling are those in which he uses the same metre as he uses prevailingly in the *Urfaust*—the Hans-Sachsian Knittelvers, the loose octo-syllabic couplets running to doggerel, with here and there irregular lines or a lyric. It is enough to recall the daring mixture of the speculative and the grotesque in *Satyros*, especially that haunting and untranslatable faun's song which Faust and Werther might have sung in unison: "Nature does homage to thee, it is all thine, thou art alone and wretched":

> Dir huldigt ringsum die Natur,
> 's ist alles dein;
> Und bist allein,
> Bist elend nur!

Or, better still, the extraordinary passage in *Der ewige Jude*, spoken by Christ on his second coming, and blending the sublime and the colloquial, the metaphysical and the urbane with the same negligent mastery as in the *Urfaust*. In this Faustian conception of Christ there is room for nature-worship, and even for a Mephistophelean aside, yet it is all done without incongruity or loss of poetic force. "O world of wondrous confusion, full of order and of slothful error, thou chain of woe and rapture, thou mother who didst bear me to the grave; whom I, though I was present at the Creation, do not understand very well on the whole":

> O Welt voll wunderbaarer Wirrung,
> Voll Geist der Ordnung, träger Irrung,
> Du Kettenring von Wonn und Wehe,
> Du Mutter die mich selbst zum Grab gebahr,
> Die ich obgleich ich bei der Schöpfung war
> Im ganzen doch nicht sonderlich verstehe.

This little-known monologue is of such power that it almost competes in merit with Faust's monologue. It has the same virtues and it takes the same liberties; and, like the *Urfaust*, it is unthinkable apart from its metre. When Goethe uses this metre he is like an educated man breaking into his local dialect with the usual gain in raciness and force. It is the style of the *Urfaust*, its poetic vernacular bristling with native associations, which gives us the surest clue to its unity and meaning. In going back to Hans Sachs, the cobbler-poet—the contemporary, by the way, not only of Luther, but of Götz and Faust as well—Goethe was going back to the oldest kind of German poetry he knew. The strictly medieval and primitive literature of the Germanic peoples was as unfamiliar to him in the seventeen-seventies as to his contemporaries, and it was quite inaccessible to him as a creative artist. Hans Sachs for the time being was the fount of German poetry, and when Goethe came on him he was like Antæus touching his Mother Earth to rise again a giant in his strength. The native note is the dominant note in the *Urfaust*, and it was the native metre that released it.

This is presumably why Goethe does not attempt to follow up his philosophical opening. In this Faustian world which he has unlocked he is incapable of developing the philosophical theme before he has vented the wealth of native association which he finds there. And so instead of a speculative poem—a maturer *Satyros* or a more dynamic *Werther*—we get, after the opening monologue, a poem of everyday life. First, the three student scenes—Faust and Wagner, Mephistopheles and the freshman, the drinking-bout in Auerbach's celler—and then the series of Gretchen scenes. Taken together, these scenes sum up with wonderful completeness the folk-life, the religious life, the student life, common alike to Goethe's day and to Luther's. They

are the direct statement in inspired poetry of the
unchanging Germany that Goethe took stock of as he
walked in the older parts of Frankfurt and Strassburg,
and looked at the faces that flitted past him and the
gabled buildings that held their shadows over him in the
narrow streets. Tavern, church, garden, and dwelling-
house; the song and the chorale; the soldier, the cleric,
the gossip; all spoke directly to him with voices of no
particular date. We are seldom reminded of a definite
epoch as we read these pages. In general character
they might be eighteenth century, they might be
fifteenth. For Goethe they were the essential and
still surviving life of older Germany, not—like *Götz
von Berlichingen*—the picturesque reconstruction of a
former age.

It is only in some such way that we can hope to grasp
the mysterious unity of this chief masterpiece of Goethe's
youth. The scenes are even more loosely connected
than in *Götz von Berlichingen*; the first scene between
Faust and the Earth-Spirit has no outward relation to
the later scenes, except that of introducing us to the
supernatural agencies which continue to operate in the
person of Mephistopheles. The student scenes which
come next are independent of one another, and none of
them is required dramatically by the Gretchen series.
And even in the Gretchen series there are scenes, such
as that introducing Valentin, or the two scenes between
Faust and Mephistopheles on the highway, which can
be omitted without disturbing the dramatic sequence.
A wonderful, an unforgettable tale is told here, but
there is no sense of a constructed plot; the poet picks
and chooses with careless freedom and almost with
caprice, and we piece the fragments together.

Yet there is a solidarity in these scenes which few
artists have achieved. They are like scattered water-
plants, floating to and fro in the upper currents of a
stream, yet securely gathered in the parental root

anchored in its bed. They are as full of outwardness as
Götz von Berlichingen; we never lose contact, as we
frequently do in *Werther*, with the tangible world. The
Gothic study, the noisy wine-cellar, the chamber with
the sanded floor, the reverberating cathedral nave, the
dungeon and the clanking chains—these things live in
our minds for ever. Yet we are never able to see them
merely as properties; we do not experience them
scenically; but only, as it were, in depth. At every point
in the text we strike downwards, and there we find the
unity which the surface of the work denies us. The
number of scenes might be halved, or it might be doubled,
the unity would be the same. It is the unity we find in
old folk-books of ballads and tales, all grown in a
common locality, and all smelling of a common soil. It
is a unity, a family unity, which Goethe alone, it may
be, among modern artists was able to create at this
pitch of intensity; and he was only able to do it once.

This may help to explain why the characters in the
Urfaust scarcely take us to the dramatist's workshop,
though they hold their own with any that have come
out of it. The figures of Gretchen and Mephistopheles,
and in their degree the slighter studies of Frau Marthe
and Lieschen and Valentin, are as vitally alive as the
best of Shakespeare's figures; yet they are somehow
un-Shakespearean, we cannot press the comparison.
If we are to compare them in kind with any of another's
making we should think rather of the immortal pair of
Cervantes', where, as in the *Urfaust*, there is an underlying folk-quality which persuades us that we are
listening to the voices of a race or a regional consciousness, voices too rich in environmental echoes and
overtones to be the product of a strictly individual
imagination. Or—and it amounts to the same thing—
the figures in the *Urfaust* do not affect us as the chance
creations of a young man's mind, but they are flesh of
his flesh and bone of his bone, too deeply rooted in

himself and in the recesses of his daily life, his background, to be separately his as Shakespeare's usually seem to be.

The *Urfaust* and *Werther* sum up between them the immediate life which Goethe lived and knew, the native environment and the spirit of nature which passed over him and through him and constituted his world. If he apprehended his world in terms of his age, and was in no trivial sense the disciple of Rousseau, Hamann, and Herder, that did not make his apprehension less immediate; it only gave it an added vitality and a firmer hold on the living present. His inspired forerunners were like a wave of natural energy, which held him aloft whilst it carried him with it. They were that part of nature which was nearest to his poetic mind, and he responded to them as he responded to the voice of the wind and the warmth of the sun.

This is precisely the difference between the Goethe who followed Shakespeare or Charlotte and the Goethe who wrote *Werther* and the *Urfaust* and the shorter lyrics and fragments that go with them. In these works he was reacting to the whole of the natural world about him, he was reacting to influences which reached him in the air that he breathed and the ground that he trod. They were influences that depended on nothing in particular, neither on the reading of a particular poet, nor on intercourse with a particular person. If they had not reached him through the channels of Herder or Sesenheim, they would have reached him through other channels. They floated about him in the atmosphere like Macbeth's dagger, or the spirits which Faust summoned: "You are hovering round me, answer if you hear":

> Ihr schwebt, ihr Geister, neben mir;
> Antwortet mir, wenn ihr mich hört,

and they could not be ignored.

But there is more than this.   If in these works Goethe found himself as a poet of nature, he not less surely found himself as a poet of self.   For if he could respond marvellously to the living environment, he could only do so by merging himself in it and making himself one with it.   His creative impulse, it seems, was all of a piece with the Werther impulse or the Faust impulse in the completeness of its demands.   It was incapable of operating smoothly by itself, it required the support of all his other faculties; it involved his whole person; so that for him the act of poetry was less an act of imagining or apprehending than of living, being, and becoming. That is why the *Urfaust*, not less than the admittedly autobiographical *Werther*, is rooted in Goethe's daily life and is in this sense intimately lyrical.   We shall not fathom Werther the better by aligning him with René, Adolphe, and his other contemporaries in European fiction, nor shall we see more deeply into the *Urfaust* by associating it with the new German drama, or with any other drama.   Drama is perhaps the lesser part of it, as fiction is the lesser part of *Werther*.

CHAPTER IV

THE SELF IN DISGUISE

WHAT holds good for *Werther* and the *Urfaust* holds good for other works—the lyrical content is seldom far to seek behind the deceptive exterior. *Torquato Tasso* is an evident case. Drama it may be in its outer garb, but it is not drama all through, nor is it exactly drama in origin. Its inception in Goethe's mind cannot have been that of normal drama, of Schiller, say, or Corneille; it must have been nearly that of the Charlotte poems which are one in spirit with it. *Egmont*, again, though probably a normal drama at first, suffered an invasion in mid-career which seriously retarded its outward movement and in the end swamped it. Here too, though not quite as in *Torquato Tasso* or the *Urfaust*, there is a personal element, a lyricism, that cannot be overlooked.

There seems to be no end to it. At every turn, in places expected and unexpected, in verse and in prose, in drama and fiction no less than in song, this ubiquitous lyricism comes to light. Must we conclude that nothing of Goethe's has escaped it, that all the works of Goethe are lyrical in their degree, even where they offer least appearance of being so?

The answer is not far from an unqualified "Yes." Of the more important works in narrative and dramatic form there are surprisingly few that can be read as such, unlyrically, as we read the narrative and drama of others. But there are just enough to show that Goethe initially possessed and never wholly lost the power to compose in this way. *Götz von Berlichingen, Hermann und Dorothea* in middle years, and the later *Wahlver-*

58

wandtschaften impress us as being essentially unlyrical. Unlike *Werther* and the rest they do not seem to have originated in states of mind that might conceivably have vented themselves in song, ode, or elegy. They do not seem to be the expression of a mood of Goethe's; they seem rather to have passed at once into action and dialogue, or at least to have quickly externalized themselves in process of writing or of gestation. There is no proof of this, but there is every probability, because we can read *Götz von Berlichingen* as we read *King John* or *Ivanhoe, Hermann und Dorothea* as we read *The Knightes Tale, Die Wahlverwandtschaften* as we read *Madame Bovary*, and nowhere does there seem to be anything in our approach which obscures our view of them.

What this means can best be seen by looking at a work of the other type. *Torquato Tasso* happens to be a very illuminating example. Although it is not typical of Goethe's philosophy and tells us little of his thoughts on man, nature, and the universe, it is very typical of the use he made of the forms of poetry. In the novel adjustment it betrays between dramatic and lyrical, between the demands of the play and the demands of self, between fable and autobiography, it is as representative of him as anything he wrote. In this sense, if not in the philosophical sense, it is most truly Goethe.

The action of *Torquato Tasso* turns chiefly on the reconciliation of Tasso the poet and Antonio the statesman, both attached to the court of Alfons, Duke of Ferrara. Alfons is dissatisfied with Tasso's behaviour, finding him aloof, suspicious, and irascible, and is eager to cure him of these vices, both in Tasso's interest as a poet needing wider experience, and in his own proprietary interest as dictator of the society about him. It is decided in consequence that Tasso must associate with Antonio, and learn from him the demeanour and the practical wisdom of the great world. Tasso in his turn is eager to serve this apprenticeship and enlarge his individuality. Unfortunately the two men are incompatible. Antonio bridles at Tasso wearing his poet's wreath in broad daylight; Tasso, quick to sense an opponent, bridles in return. The outcome of their first private conference is that Tasso draws his sword on Antonio and is put in temporary confinement by Alfons, while Antonio, who retains his freedom, is entrusted with the burden of reconciliation. A second conference, more amicable than the first but equally ineffective, leaves Tasso unreformed; his next act is to forget himself unpardonably before the Princess, Alfons's sister, and to complete his humiliation by throwing himself into her arms like a schoolboy. His folly is observed, and he stands disgraced. At the last he is left clinging to Antonio as a drowning man clings to a straw.

This is one of the least convincing, the least satisfactory plots in dramatic literature. It is not, like many plots in romantic or comic drama, a fantastically unreal one, made acceptable by a continual outpouring of beauty or merriment. Nor are we merely faced with the occasional contradictions which we expect to find in plots dependent on motive. The plot is of the latter variety; it is based on social life and the play of character, and it invites, or seems to invite, the same kind of scrutiny as, let us say, *Othello* or *Hedda Gabler*. Yet if we make this scrutiny the play collapses. It collapses because there is an inconsistency at the heart of it, an inconsistency which the spirit of the play thrusts before us.

Tact, discretion, the nuances of conversation, the fine points of social intercourse—these are the life-breath of the play, and the Princess, who sets the pace in the early scenes, is the embodiment of them. "If you would learn the exact bounds of the permissible, inquire of noble women. For they are most concerned that only the permissible should happen. The walls of propriety encircle their tender sex. Where propriety rules, they rule. And where rudeness enters, they are nothing":

> Willst du genau erfahren, was sich ziemt,
> So frage nur bei edlen Frauen an.
> Denn ihnen ist am meisten dran gelegen,
> Das alles wohl sich zieme, was geschieht.
> Die Schicklichkeit umgibt mit einer Mauer
> Das zarte, leicht verletzliche Geschlecht.
> Wo Sittlichkeit regiert, regieren sie,
> Und wo die Frechheit herrscht, da sind sie nichts.

This, we might say, is the discipline in which Tasso proves himself her imperfect pupil. For if we except the faint scruples, voiced once or twice, as to the justice of exonerating Antonio—"I hardly know which of the two is to blame," says the Princess confidentially to Leonore—the offence rests solely on Tasso, and the rest of them, Antonio included, go scot-free. Alfons appears throughout as the judicious ruler, not in a syllable is his discretion impugned; and the Princess falls in with his scheme as readily as the others, saying frankly to Tasso: "You must be friends. I flatter myself that I can quickly bring this fair event to pass." If only we could fall in with the scheme too! But the truth is that the treatment of Tasso by these friends and well-wishers of his will scarcely bear looking at. Judged alike by the fastidious standards of the play and the mother-wit of the average reader, this treatment is ill-advised and foredoomed to failure. When Alfons, hearing of Antonio's arrival hard upon Tasso's attack of poetic ecstasy, says, "It is well, he has come at the right moment," we are not convinced, and it is only when the Princess begins to voice her belated suspicions that all is not well and to fear that the whole thing is a mistake that we feel in hearty accord with her. For, as she says somewhere to Leonore, the incompatibility of the two is written in their outward bearing. "Look at the two of them, their faces, their expression, the way they walk. Everything conflicts. They can never come together":

> Sieh das Äussre nur
> Von beiden an, das Angesicht, den Ton,
> Den Blick, den Tritt. Es widerstrebt sich alles,
> Sie können ewig keine Liebe wechseln.

And while we agree with her here, we can only ask why she of all people—she the mistress of conduct and decorum—should be so slow to see it and, as the event shows, so incapable of acting on it.

This is the central and, as it seems, almost invidious contradiction in the play—its niceties, its fine discriminations are all grouped around a situation which is little short of clumsy; the leading characters are false to themselves in a test case. Moreover, it is not a situation which we can close our eyes to. It confronts us throughout. It is initiated early, and it continues to the end. Tasso's drawn sword does not terminate it, for Antonio is immediately thrust on him again at Alfons's command. Futile as their intercourse is—it is not too much to say that Tasso's self-control declines steadily under it—it outlasts the five acts; for the fifth act leaves them talking, and if the sixth could be written it would have to end either with Tasso's death or with the prospect of some yet more exasperated conversations between this irreconcilable pair. A playful reader might be tempted to remark that the uncertain friendship of the cat and the dog may have the making of a good fable in it, but scarcely lends itself to a five-act drama.

Some such remark is inevitable if we stick to the dramatic view, and read the work solely in terms of an external plot enacted by separate personalities. But this, after all, is a partial view; the flaw we have detected is too obvious to be explained in this way. There must be some excuse, some reason which the dramatic view misses, and if we look for it we quickly find it. To see where the reason lies, we have only to take the hint which is palpably offered that Goethe was less interested in the separate Tasso and the separate Antonio than in the interplay between them. If, owing to some problem or dilemma of his, these two characters were more closely and arbitrarily associated in his mind than drama allows, if he had a sense of personal identity with the pair of them—not with Tasso alone, or with Antonio alone, but with both together, with what we might call Tasso-Antonio—and if this sense was so strong that his interest in the scenes and events which surrounded them depended on their meeting constantly, coming together and going apart and coming together again, the whole work is changed under our eyes, its central situation becomes comprehensible, and the strange behaviour of the characters ceases to be absurd.

This interpretation has the strongest biographical support. The years in which *Torquato Tasso* was conceived and pondered were those in which Goethe felt most acutely the clash, which he never finally resolved, between the poet in him and the man of affairs. He had nipped a popular literary career in the bud in 1775 when he escaped to Weimar, and in Weimar he had assumed a burden of official duties which threatened to overwhelm him. He had yielded to a practical ambition which at the same time he disliked. He sat alternately at his ministerial desk and at the feet of Charlotte, to whom he wrote in 1783: "Here in the thick of my official business I am so chock-full of passions, hobbies, inventions, ideas, caprices, and plans that really life is often a burden to me." The more we know of this period of Goethe's life the clearer does it become that the Tasso-Antonio conflict or something closely resembling it was with him continually and haunted him day and night.

All this is common knowledge. And while the play cannot give us the clue in so many words, it does its best. Leonore says, soon after Tasso has drawn his sword against Antonio, that, as she has long felt, the two are enemies "because Nature did not make one man of them"; she says that they should seek to repair Nature's mistake by joining in friendship, "then they would stand as one man" and be like the gods of life:

> Zwei Männer sind's, ich hab' es lang' gefühlt,
> Die darum Feinde sind, weil die Natur
> Nicht *einen* Mann aus ihnen beiden formte.
> Und wären sie zu ihrem Vorteil klug,
> So würden sie als Freunde sich verbinden:
> Dann stünden sie für *einen* Mann und gingen
> Mit Macht und Glück und Lust durchs Leben hin.

Could anything be less plausible at this moment? And coming from the worldly Leonore? A more careful dramatist would at least have entrusted these lines to another, to the masterful Alfons or, better, to the speculative and esoteric Princess. But they would be dramatically unconvincing, whoever said them. Argue as we may about complementary characters and the attraction of opposites, we do not find that friendship can be manufactured on this basis, and we are astonished that the two women cling to the idea even after it has proved itself bankrupt. This is a passage which we only accept dramatically because we are used to it and take it for granted. Or perhaps it is nearer the mark to say that we do not accept it dramatically, but we accept it poetically because we feel that it somehow "belongs" and must be accepted. And to this extent we are obeying a right instinct. It does belong, but it belongs lyrically, as the expression of Goethe's private need and congenital bond with his twin-creation, rather than dramatically, as a piece of impartial commentary and character-drawing.

This one example is enough. The action of *Torquato Tasso*, unconvincing and a little ridiculous when we try to base it on the play of motive and character, becomes

inevitable when we recognize that it is at the mercy of a
lyrical dictatorship, which insists that, come what may,
salvation or shipwreck, Tasso and Antonio must constantly meet and react to one another. Alfons commands
it, the Princess and Leonore comply weakly, Antonio is
a model of obedience—and all because Goethe must have
it so if the play is to continue. It is as if these characters
dimly realized that their lives were at stake and bowed
to the inevitable.

This is the spirit in which the work asks to be read.
There is scarcely a point at which it does not gain
immeasurably. Take the closing scene. Tasso is beside
himself with self-torture and humiliation, and Antonio,
even the mollified Antonio of the later acts, would
scarcely seem the desirable counsellor at this juncture.
But Goethe, the tyrant, ruthlessly throws them together
and dispatches the rest of the company by carriage to
Ferrara. They are now quite alone and gradually
reach the note of reconciliation upon which the play
ends. It is an inconclusive and, in the dramatic view,
an incompetent ending. Yet it is a right ending. We
have only to remember that the play owes its intensity,
and perhaps its existence, to a problem of Goethe's
which outlived the writing of it to see that the ending
is justified. The work may disappoint us at the last if
we hanker after the dramatic, but it is never for a moment
unfaithful to the lyrical source upon which it has drawn
from the beginning. Only by a sort of concession to
drama does the poem come to an end at all. It might
have gone on indefinitely, as in some degree it went on
for Goethe, and this is how we think of it afterwards.

But when the most has been done for it, this final
scene is perplexing. What makes it curiously so is that
there are two easily discernible stopping-places, either
of which might have been used to end the play. First
Tasso, taking the barest hint from Antonio, awakens to
a sense of his self-sufficiency as a poet; he remembers

F

that he is endowed with noble gifts and singled out among men.   If the play had ended here with Tasso's immortal words, "While others are mute in their agony it was given to me to say what I suffer ":

> Und wenn der Mensch in seiner Qual verstummt,
> Gab mir ein Gott, zu sagen, wie ich leide,

few would have taken exception.   But no.   Goethe is not ready to stop.   Antonio in his turn reasserts himself and reaches his hand to Tasso who, soon forgetting the new-found source of strength within him, collapses and throws himself on his companion, like the sailor who "clings to the rock on which he was shipwrecked ":

> So klammert sich der Schiffer endlich noch
> Am Felsen fest, an dem er scheitern sollte.

It is true that Tasso, like Werther, switches incalculably from one extreme to the other, and Antonio has reminded us of this shortly before.   Yet even with his assistance this sudden twist at the very end of the play is hard to accept.   If Goethe were content to be Tasso-Antonio all the time it would ease things.   But it is clear that he is Tasso-Antonio at one moment—when contrary to all expectation the one figure suddenly clutches at the other—and Tasso alone the moment before—when the poet remembers his birthright in words that are so intimately Goethe's—words which were wrung from him again in old age in the most agonized of all his lyrical poems, the "Trilogie der Leidenschaft."

This makes for a difficult piece of poetry.   It means that in order to get the full value out of the last moments of the play we have to shift quickly from identifying Goethe with one of his characters to identifying him with two.   Nor is this all.   It is not enough that Goethe is sometimes Tasso and sometimes Tasso-Antonio, there are moments when he forgets himself and lets Tasso become conscious of Tasso-Antonio. After their first meeting Tasso confesses that Antonio's nature and conversation have affected him strangely, he says that he feels more "dual and divided (doppelt) than ever," and that "he is plunged again into turmoil and conflict with himself":

> Sein Wesen, seine Worte haben mich
> So wunderbar getroffen, dass ich mehr
> Als je mich doppelt fühle, mit mir selbst
> Aufs neu' in streitender Verwirrung bin.

The case is plain. The problem which Goethe is conveying dramatically by means of the whole play, and more especially by the clash of two of his characters, here creeps unawares into the mind of one of the two. There is no urgent need for Tasso to describe himself in terms of such explicit dualism; if these strange words of his were left unsaid, we should not miss them. It is Goethe, not Tasso, who is dual at this moment and, to be strictly consistent, he should not use Tasso to say it. Indeed, it is essential that Tasso, having said it, should forget it again, because in the deeper intention of the play he is, with Antonio, the dramatic and unconscious expression of it.

This is confusing, yet it is not to be wondered at. It was only to be expected that the poet-dramatist, lapsing from complex lyricism into simple, should occasionally throw in with his poet-hero, if only for the reason that both are poets. Besides, there is the more vital consideration that in respect of another character, the Princess, it is Tasso, and Tasso alone, who is Goethe. For, as we have seen, Tasso stands to the Princess exactly as Goethe stood to Charlotte.

This is the other half—already noted—of the poem's lyricism. While it is not less potent than the first, it has a different function, and only rarely conflicts with it. Dramatically, the Antonio theme is dominant and the Princess theme is subordinate to it, Tasso's final humiliation in love being used in the development of the plot to force upon him the necessity of relying on

Antonio. But in another sense it is the reverse of
subordinate. The Princess—voice of Charlotte—is the
poetic mistress of the play, and it is from her, or from
her and Tasso, that it draws its atmosphere and texture.
The Princess theme supplies the spirit of the play, and
the Antonio theme supplies the action. Tasso belongs
to both, being all Goethe in relation to the Princess, and
part Goethe in relation to Antonio. But sometimes this
difference is forgotten, and by a slight inconsistency he
becomes all Goethe in the latter case. Hence, in its
subtler implication, the dual mood which creeps on him
now and then, and for the moment displaces Antonio.

This is one way of reading *Torquato Tasso*. There is
nothing hard and fast in it, and there can be no finality
of interpretation. But as to the general character of
the poem and its relation to normal drama some agree-
ment is possible. *Torquato Tasso* is a work of drama,
yet not wholly of drama. The figures are not consistently cast from the dramatist's lantern upon the
external screen and held there, but they withdraw
through his magic lens—we never quite know when—
and become one with him for a while; then they leave
him again, though we never see them return. Or it
may be that he, their creator, follows them occasionally
and enters this one or that of the antic figures, yet he
moves as invisibly into the picture and out again as
they do. Some figures there are who always stay on the
screen; others have a way of flitting on and off together
as if in obedience to some law, not apparent, which
makes them converge on each other. We cannot see all
this, we can only infer the nature of the creative process
from what the screen pictures tell us. The figures behave
strangely, even unintelligibly at first, yet they never
seem to get out of hand.

If it is asked by what authority a poet plays havoc
with the accepted forms and writes a drama which is
thus capriciously and imperfectly detached from his

private life—a drama in which the characters obey two sets of laws, not fully reconcilable, and, when in doubt, obey the inner and unacknowledged laws of the poet's consanguinity with them rather than the avowed laws of the dramatic action—there can be no ready answer. Goethe's works are full of this kind of liberty, we cannot imagine his poetry without it.   Tasso is merely one example—a highly subtle and complex example— among many.

One only needs to look at the shorter poems to see this.   Just as *Torquato Tasso*, the supposed drama, is controlled, even in its structure and movement, by lyrical impulses, so the supposed lyrics are continually passing over into ballad and drama and disguising themselves in external forms.   The consequence is that the dividing-line which is often drawn for convenience between lyrics and ballads is both flimsy and misleading; the ballad may be more personal in inspiration than the lyric.   Thus the famous "Heidenröslein," which passes commonly as an impersonal treatment in song or ballad form of a theme from folk-poetry, probably owes its existence among Goethe's works to his reading of the old theme in terms of himself and Friederike—a consideration which supports the view, now in favour, though not absolutely proved, that Goethe was the author, the re-creator, of this little masterpiece and not, as it is just possible to argue, merely the subtle retoucher of it.   In this case the question of a partially veiled lyricism bears directly on the question of authorship.

The ballad, "Der Fischer," telling of the angler who is decoyed into the stream by the waterfay and drowned, betrays a similar complexity.   No sooner was it written than Herder put it into his collection of folk-poems and acclaimed it a model of its kind.   If German poetry, he said, was to recover its folk appeal it must follow in the footsteps of this poem.   To-day, a hundred and fifty years later, we can read the poem as Herder read it—

impersonally—and endorse his judgment.   Yet we know also—this did not interest Herder—that there is another side to the story.   The love-note in this poem, especially evident in the lines, "The water roared, the water rose, and wetted his naked foot; his heart yearned as at his loved one's greeting":

> Das Wasser rauscht', das Wasser schwoll,
> Netzt' ihm den nackten Fuss;
> Sein Herz wuchs ihm so sehnsuchtsvoll,
> Wie bei der Liebsten Gruss,

is somehow connected with the moon-lyric, "An den Mond," and particularly with the strange words from its first draft, "Under your spell this burning, restless heart of mine haunts the stream like a ghost":

> Das du so beweglich kennst,
> Dieses Herz in Brand,
> Haltet ihr wie ein Gespenst
> An den Fluss gebannt.

The exact details will never be known.   The suicide of Christiane von Lasberg, who leapt into the Ilm with *Werther* in her pocket, may have contributed something, though this is uncertain; the personal relation with Charlotte von Stein was probably all-important.   For our purpose it is enough to recognize the very great likelihood that one of the most unfathomably personal of Goethe's lyrics and one of his most successful folk-ballads are intimately associated in origin.

Thus what we have seen in the case of *Torquato Tasso* and other longer works holds good for the short works —we never know precisely where the lyricism begins or where it ends, or what form it will take.   Even the complex lyricism may assert itself in what seems the simplest of poems.   Perhaps the earliest case of the dual mood is the unassuming little fable "Adler und Taube," written in the early seventies.   An eagle is wounded by an arrow and loses the use of its wings; but a dove, seeing it crawling on the ground, comforts it with a

picture of the quieter consolations which are all the
dove knows, and which the eagle can still share with it.
It is tempting at a glance to interpret this little parable
as expressing the conflict between the new school of
poets and the quiet bourgeoisie—Genie und harmloser
Philister—and in this sense to see Goethe in the eagle
and some easy-going unideal interlocutor in the dove.
Yet this is to simplify the case too much. The stronger
probability is that Goethe is himself both dove and
eagle, and that even at this early date he is communing
dramatically with himself, the eagle being the voice of
the universal aspiration which spends itself elsewhere in
Werther's musings, the rapture of Ganymede, and the
ambition of Faust, and the dove the voice of contentment
and control which Werther heeded too little and Goethe,
as some think, heeded too well. This, if the accent and
the beauty of the words are to be trusted, is Goethe's
true relation to his poem. For how with any mere
Philistinism in mind could he have put its most delicate
lines into the dove's pleadings? "You wander through
the dewy flowers, take your chosen food from the woodland plenty, quench your mild thirst at the silver spring":

> Du wandelst durch der Blumen frischen Tau,
> Pflückst aus dem Überfluss
> Des Waldgebüsches dir
> Gelegne Speise, letzest
> Den leichten Durst am Silberquell.

This dualism, elementary in the fable of dove and
eagle, highly complex in Tasso and Antonio, does not
produce the ordinary type of dialogue. The ordinary
type—the type we may call "imaginary conversations"
—begins in dialogue and ends in dialogue. The author,
let us say, is attracted by a pair of historical, legendary,
or invented figures, and sets them talking together; his
personality may colour his choice and interfere with
the conversation, but for the most part they retain their
seeming independence. The author's purpose is to let

them talk; he may have a theory to insinuate, but, if he has, he will do his best to let it come from them and not from him. This, in simple statement, is what dialogue usually means.

Goethe's typical pairs of figures impress us differently. Either by the accents of their speech or by a strangeness in their behaviour, they betray their common origin; they signal to us by some means or other that they are not just Tasso and Antonio, Faust and Mephistopheles, Prometheus and Epimetheus, and what not, but that they are strings of one instrument, branches of one tree, limbs of one person. We may not discover it at once, but sooner or later there is no missing it. The left hand may act as if it did not know what the right hand was doing, but it always comes out that they have acted in connivance, obedient to a single will and a single personality. The ear learns to detect the self-communion behind the debate, the monologue behind the dialogue.

Moreover we find that these pairs of figures, unlike the branches of the tree with which we have just compared them, are continually striving to grow together again. Either they join forces and become inseparable, like Faust and Mephistopheles, or they struggle towards friendship like Tasso and Antonio, or they part tragically like Werther and Albert, or in some fashion they make us feel that, whether they admit it or not, they need one another. For, clearly, with a drop of Albert in his veins Werther would have found a means of living, while Mephistopheles, equally clearly, is a preservative element in his partner's life—the salt, as it were, of the Faustian existence. The simile of the tree and the branches is not enough, we need that of the divided river which becomes one, its two arms driven from their common bed only to seek and find it again.

It is not for nothing that Goethe carried the theme of his "Paria" in mind for half a lifetime before setting it down on paper. "Paria" is the latest and intensest expression of his ever-changing dualism, just as the fable of the eagle and the dove is the earliest and gentlest. The story is that of the Brahmin's wife who fetches water daily from the sacred Ganges, carrying it, by virtue of her miraculous purity, as a ball of crystal in her arms. Her soul's mirror being one day dimmed at the critical moment, her power leaves her, and the water slips idly through her fingers. In her husband's eyes she stands convicted of sin; he drags her to the place of graves and beheads her. Their son now assures his father of his mother's innocence and threatens to follow her to the grave, but the father tells him that it is not too late, he can still put head and body together, and they will resume their former life. But in his haste the son joins his mother's head to the body of a pariah, creating in this way a monstrous hybrid, torn by insane conflicts, half angel, half outcast. Thus is the basest of mankind redeemed, and son and father go forth to tell it among men.

Goethe's interest in this theme may have been less in its humanitarianism than in the psychology of its central figure, the dual monster alternating between divine illumination and blind frenzy. This is a different dualism from any that he had expressed before, it is more tragic and more elemental. "And so I, the Brahmin, dwelling with my head in heaven, shall feel as a pariah the downward pull of earth":

> Und so soll ich, die Brahmane,
> Mit dem Haupt im Himmel weilend,
> Fühlen, Paria, dieser Erde
> Niederziehende Gewalt.

It differs also in that it achieves the union in one body of what before was the life of two; it achieves this tragically, but the achievement brings immense benefits to man. The bearing of this terrifying narrative on Goethe's poetic mind is not to be summed up lightly.

But for our immediate purpose it will be agreed that
no theme in the whole realm of fable could have furnished
him with so powerful a symbol of dualism seeking unity,
and it brings home to us as nothing else could the
urgency of the lyrical impulse which turned the dove
to the eagle, and thrust Tasso upon Antonio.

Yet in none of these instances is Goethe's lyricism
extended to the full. We see that it readily breaks into
two voices and, if we look at *Torquato Tasso* again, we
can see that it readily breaks into several. For in one
way or another all the characters in *Torquato Tasso* are
Goethe—first Tasso himself and the Princess, who are
the dramatic equivalent of a lyric to Charlotte; then
Antonio, the symbol of Goethe's public ambition. And
if we take from the two remaining characters what they
share with these three, there is little or nothing left.
Leonore is not consistently differentiated from the
Princess and frequently speaks in accents not distin-
guishable from hers, while Alfons, the controlling agent,
pulls the strings for Goethe, and that is all. He merely
stands for Goethe's determination to bring Tasso and
Antonio together and is in no sense a serious study of
Karl August or of any ruler. When Goethe wished to
draw the character of his patron he wrote the poem
"Ilmenau," beside which the character of Alfons fades
into unreality. Neither in Alfons nor in Leonore is
there anything to interest us apart from the assistance
they give in sustaining and elucidating the lyrically
created central situation. In this light Tasso is a lyric
expanded into drama, and it is nothing else.

But it is a somewhat rarefied Goethe who speaks to
us through this play. His personality fills the play, yet
we do not feel the full weight of his personality. If in
comparative restraint and quietude he can reach this
variety of self-utterance, how far can he be drawn by a
larger and more resonant theme? The answer to this
question is in the completed *Faust*.

CHAPTER V

IT is easy to forget that *Faust* is Goethe's poem first
and Germany's afterwards; the theme of it is so
large, its affiliations with the national mind so constant
and so inexhaustible. Like certain great poems of
antiquity *Faust* seems to epitomize a civilization, it is
German in the almost mythological sense that it rises
as a legend from the dark background of German life
and has all the German mind and German character
in it. What is more reasonable than to assume that
Goethe was alive to its representative aspect from the
start; that he allowed this aspect to have weight with
him in committing himself to a Faust poem; and that
it was this that kept him wrestling with it intermittently
to the end of his days? Why should a man strive for
two generations with so overpowering a theme unless
he is actuated by some sense of mission and service,
some such promptings, let us say, as made Virgil write
his *Æneid*, or Spenser his *Faerie Queene*?

At first sight everything points to it. Yet it was not
so. National considerations can have meant but little
to Goethe; we can be certain that if he ever entertained
any such thoughts concerning *Faust* he quickly dismissed
them. If *Faust* has become a sort of secular bible, if it
has so impressed itself on the German people that its
lines have passed wholesale into the common language,
that is more in spite of Goethe's intention than because
of it. His sole active interest in *Faust* was in relation
to himself; from first to last he bent it resolutely to his
private need, and it was only by doing so that he was
able to reach the end. The poem owes its existence to

75

this personal relation with it; its national qualities came unforced and unsought.

We have seen the beginnings of this personal relation, this stealthy partnership between poet and poem, in the *Urfaust*. We have seen how directly the *Urfaust* gives voice to Goethe's native sense of the world about him, and how imperceptibly it merges into *Werther* and the early nature lyrics. What is less easy but not less important to see is that the lyricism of the *Urfaust* pervades the whole of it, and is as strong at the end, in the Gretchen tragedy, as at the beginning. If we examine the whole of Goethe's output at this time— say from the summer in Wetzlar to his departure for Weimar—we find it impossible to draw any sure line between lyrical and non-lyrical. From dithyrambic monologues and simple outbursts of song we pass to dramatic and narrative fragments filled with rhapsodic self-expression, and from these to *Werther* and the *Urfaust*—one a novel and the other a tragedy, but held together by innumerable links of imagery, phrase, vocabulary which we can readily trace back to the lyrics proper and identify as tokens of Goethe's personal feeling. All these works, we discover, spring from a common reservoir of lyrical emotion. Excepting *Götz von Berlichingen*, which just antedates this period, and *Egmont*, which all but post-dates it—both of them less inscrutable productions based on historical sources— we can say that almost everything Goethe wrote in these years came from him like an emanation, a welling-up from within of the new life that had awakened in him. If part of this self-expression is complex and assumes the form of myth or legend, that is only because, as later in *Torquato Tasso*, it is too rich to voice itself in simple melody. The myth is, so to speak, the partial orchestration of a theme first written or intended for the solo instrument. Never do we suspect that the lyrical inspiration is inadequate, or that it has been suppressed. The use of drama—as in the *Prometheus* fragment—usually deepens and intensifies the lyrical voice. And if this flow of lyricism, divinely enraptured at some points, is tragic at others, and in one instance —the close of the Gretchen tragedy in the *Urfaust*— reaches an intensity of suffering which we can only compare with the greatest moments in drama, even this does not mean that Goethe's inspiration has shifted from lyrical to non-lyrical, it simply tells of a lyricism too intense for anything less strenuous than tragedy. The lyricism breaks into tragedy much as Werther's ecstasy breaks into horror; it is like the lightning whose fitful illuminations, as they come nearer, grow more and more ominous till at last they blind and annihilate.

The completed *Faust* brings this out in a practical way. When Goethe came to strengthen the dramatic or narrative link between the prison-scene, the close of the Gretchen tragedy, and the opening monologue in Faust's study—the *Urfaust* had been content to leave these two scenes carelessly bound in a loose sheaf with others—all he had to do was to develop the theme lyrically stated in the first of the two. The sequence is briefly this. Faust, foiled incessantly in his insatiable yearning for more than partial knowledge, has renounced the intellectual approach. "Here I stand," he says, "poor fool that I am, just as wise as I was before":

> Da steh' ich nun, ich armer Tor!
> Und bin so klug als wie zuvor.

But when he tries the magic or mystic approach he finds himself defeated again; the vision of the vast Earth-Spirit, which he evokes crushes him with the thought of his inadequacy. Thus far the *Urfaust*, which, after disposing of these two approaches to the universal, turns to less philosophical scenes, leaving it to the completed First Part to carry its broken speculations farther. First there is added the suicide scene, dramatically

induced by motives of despair, but in the event consti-
tuting a third approach, Werther's approach this time,
to life untrammelled. "This exalted life, this godlike
rapture!"

> Dies hohe Leben, diese Götterwonne!

says Faust with the poison at his lips. And then the
compact with Mephistopheles, again prompted by
despair, and again turning under the stress of Faust's
invincible idealism into one more avenue to the all and
absolute. Mephistopheles, to be sure, deprecates this
view of it and suggests the imaginative approach as an
obvious alternative. "Get into partnership with a poet,"
he says:

> Assoziiert euch mit einem Poeten.

But it is characteristic of Faust, and of Goethe's poetic
mind too, that he ignores this proposal and will have
nothing short of the full experience of mankind, quanti-
tatively. "All that is allotted to mankind I will savour
in person, touch with my spirit the highest and lowest,
heap on myself man's weal and woe, and thus expand
myself into humanity's self and, like humanity, smash
up in the end":

> Und was der ganzen Menschheit zugeteilt ist,
> Will ich in meinem innern Selbst geniessen,
> Mit meinem Geist das Höchst' und Tiefste greifen,
> Ihr Wohl und Weh auf meinen Busen häufen,
> Und so mein eigen Selbst zu ihrem Selbst erweitern,
> Und, wie sie selbst, am End' auch ich zerscheitern.

And now, with little delay, the Gretchen tragedy follows
as the first notable application of Faust's violent ambition
ot his experience of the world and men.

There is nothing in the rest of the completed First
Part that cannot be read in terms of Goethe. Both the
Easter Sunday walk (Vor dem Tor), and the night on
the Brocken (Walpurgisnacht)—to name two of the

more important additions—fall readily into place in the
native world of the *Urfaust*. No doubt they are more
coolly and deliberately executed, they do not pulse like
the older scenes. But they excellently round off the
poetic summary of Goethe's early world which the older
scenes began, and there can be no satisfactory explanation of them which ignores this view. Neither of them
is required dramatically, since Faust could have met
Mephistopheles without the one, and Gretchen could
have got to the scaffold without the other; while as
narrative scenes they obviously over-weight and over-
retard an exciting tale, the Walpurgisnacht being in this
respect a notorious offender.

If we reject the native explanation of them as scenes
representative of Goethe's environment—one a simple
transcript of the German people on holiday, the other a
summing-up of traditional superstitions—we are driven
back on the more casual explanation which says that
Goethe was willing to make *Faust* the repository for
anything he chose, "a garbage-can and a lumber-
room" (ein Kehrichtfass und eine Rumpelkammer),
and that we must not look for poetic logic in so loose and
comprehensive a work. This is at first sight a plausible
explanation, the plan of the poem is all-inclusive,
theoretically Goethe could throw into it what he liked.
But those who read *Faust* in this spirit forget that
Goethe could only like what he intimately knew and felt,
and that he had merely escaped the discipline of a close
plot and an architectural technique to fall into the
clutches of a discipline far more inexorable. For all its
apparent confusion *Faust* has its poetic logic no less than
the *Divine Comedy* or *Paradise Lost*. Capricious it may
seem on a first reading, but it is not really so, for there is
nothing in it which is not intimately Goethe's by virtue
of long association or intense emotional experience, and
there is nothing in it that does not square with the
legend and its traditions. The Walpurgisnachtstraum

—a possible exception—can be said to prove the rule.
The poem may look formless to an eye that comes to it
from Racine or Dante, yet there is this curiously exacting
double check on it at every point—it can only include
what is at one and the same time germane to the myth
and personal to the poet. This makes it, with all its
appearance of laxity and notwithstanding a flagrant
breach here and there, the severest of Goethe's works;
it explains why he found it hardest to write and took
longest to write it.

To tell the whole story of this adjustment of autobiography to myth and myth to autobiography would fill
volumes. It begins with the earliest scenes, written in
youth, and it persists to the latest scenes, written
in extreme age. The adjustment may become less
spontaneous as time goes by, but it does not become less
close. If Goethe opens the Second Part with the con-
valescence of Faust on an Alpine meadow and passes
from there by rapid stages to a Florentine masquerade,
in which the Greek mythological figures of Fates, Furies,
and Graces appear in costume, sounding the Classical
note lightly and letting it die away again, to be followed
in due course by the demand for Helena, crassly at first
to suit the whim of an emperor, but gravely and deliberately afterwards in consequence of Faust's newly
awakened desire for her—what is this but the statement
in poetic terms of Goethe's contact with Italy and with
the Classicism which he associated with Italy? All the
essentials are there—the tentative journeys to Switzerland prior to crossing the Alps, the superficial Classicism
dating from his Leipzig days, the slow search for a deeper
Classicism by dint of study, science, and long travel,
until at last it became his and he made Helena a reality,
only to lose her again, yet not wholly to lose her, in the
onflowing of life. We can trace it all in these wonderfully
consistent pages. Yet in translating his middle years
into these high Faustian symbols Goethe was doing no

violence to the legend. The union of Faust and Helena dated from the earliest chap-books, and it was incumbent on him, Classicist or no Classicist, to do what he could with it.

Needless to say, this constant dependence on autobiography, this lyricism, has a vital bearing on the character of the poem. We have only to remember what happened in *Torquato Tasso*. Such, we found, was the degree of lyrical interference in *Torquato Tasso* that it not only deprived the characters of the liberty usually accorded in drama, but it made them behave in ways that drama cannot account for; they were not, it proved on examination, really independent personalities, each with a mind and a will of his own, but they were continually at the mercy of the ruling mind and will that made them; they might seem at times to be the individual voices which we expected them to be, but in reality they merged or were ready at any moment to merge in the lyrical voice which dominated and included them all. In a final view this play is not so much a study of several minds as the study of one mind imposing itself on several; it is less a drama than a monologue, radiating, as it were, into drama.

In *Faust* this condition is repeated on an immense scale. Just as Tasso, Antonio, and the rest were incongruous so long as we insisted on treating them as separate entities and only lost their incongruity when we saw that they were the constituent parts of a single entity, so it is with Faust, Mephistopheles, and the motley figures among which they move—they are all channels for the one lyrical impulse to flow through. They are all component parts of Goethe, and they must be read accordingly. This is the law of *Faust*, as it was the law of *Torquato Tasso*.

Take the famous passage in which Faust, like a modern Job, roundly curses life and the world in the ears of Mephistopheles, ending with: "Cursed be the wine that

G

soothes, cursed the supreme graciousness of love!
Cursed be hope, and faith, and patience most of all":

> Fluch sei dem Balsamsaft der Trauben!
> Fluch jener höchsten Liebeshuld!
> Fluch sei der Hoffnung! Fluch dem Glauben,
> Und Fluch vor allen der Geduld!

No sooner has his titanic outburst spent itself in a mental
shattering of all that is dear to the heart and the senses
—the charm of the outer world, pride of mind, fame,
property, wealth, and even these highest virtues and
rewards—than a chorus of invisible spirits, speaking in
accents of great aerial beauty, deplores his act of
spiritual nihilism and bids him restore what he has
undone. "Alas, alas! thou hast destroyed the world
with a mighty hand. It falls and crumbles. A demi-
god has shattered it. We carry its ruins into the void
and lament the beauty lost. Mighty son of earth,
rebuild it in thy heart, begin a new life with freshened
mind, and let new songs be sung to it":

> Weh! Weh!
> Du hast sie zerstört,
> Die schöne Welt,
> Mit mächtiger Faust,
> Sie stürzt, sie zerfällt!
> Ein Halbgott hat sie zerschlagen!
> Wir tragen
> Die Trümmern ins Nichts hinüber
> Und klagen
> Über die verlorne Schöne.
> Mächtiger
> Der Erdensöhne,
> Prächtiger
> Baue sie wieder,
> In deinem Busen baue sie auf.
> Neuen Lebenslauf
> Beginne,
> Mit hellem Sinne,
> Und neue Lieder
> Tönen darauf!

Mephistopheles now claims that the spirits are servants of his, whose monitions Faust would do well to heed. "These," he says, "are some of my lesser attendants. Note how precociously they urge you to enjoy life and be active. They would fain entice you out of this stagnant solitude into the wide world":

> Dies sind die Kleinen
> Von den Meinen.
> Höre, wie zu Lust und Taten
> Altklug sie raten!
> In die Welt weit,
> Aus der Einsamkeit,
> Wo Sinnen und Säfte stocken,
> Wollen sie dich locken.

Dramatically the passage is perplexing. What are these spirits? Are they, like those in the previous scene, really the minions of Mephistopheles, or is he adroitly claiming them on the spur of the moment? If they are his, why do they show such unfeigned moral consternation? The questions multiply and, if we read the passage strictly as drama, they have to be asked. Yet there is no satisfactory answer to them, and the reason is that the work itself does not ask them; it is we who ask them. If instead of clinging to the dramatic interpretation we read the passage lyrically as a sequence of moods or impulses incidental to one mind rather than to several, these perplexities disappear and there is nothing obscure. Faust vents his curse, the brazen bell of his frenzy ceases to clang, and in the pause that follows we hear the reverberations, the inner reverberations, in the mind of the curser. The transition from Faust's words to the spirit's words does not take us from one mind to another, it simply registers a change in one and the same mind—the remorse after the curse, the reaction after the excess, the inevitable flowing onward of the consciousness.

This must be the meaning of the passage, because it is

what every sensitive reader goes through when he
submits to it, so that whatever the printed page says or
suggests we have no choice but to identify these spirit-
voices with the surging consciousness of Faust. But
this is not all. When Mephistopheles says that they are
his, we have to admit that in some degree they are;
psychologically he has a claim on them, as well as
Faust, since their summons back to life leads the mind
at once to thoughts of the sensuous world—as contrasted
with the darkness of the curse—and the Mephistophelean
undertone of seductiveness insinuates itself quite spontaneously at such a moment. When we say that these
lines, which in the text are divided among various
spokesmen, are the expression of an intense passage in
the life of a single consciousness we are putting the only
interpretation on them which our experience of them
will support. Thus it is not so much Faust's mind
which despairs and relents as the mind of the poem, the
total mind, the one mind, speaking through Faust, the
spirits, and Mephistopheles in turn.

   Read in this light, the passage is both lucid and satisfying. There is no need to argue as to the precise degree
of separateness which the poet—here or elsewhere—
allows to his figures; the compromise between the
dramatic and the lyrical requirements of the poem is
flexible and must be taken flexibly. It is enough if
we recognize that the dramatic requirements, however
strong, are subordinate. Yet without the use of drama
Goethe could never have said so much; it is inconceivable
that he could have rendered this passage of emotional
life with the same fullness and intensity if he had
kept to simple lyrical forms. The legendary powers of
Faust and Mephistopheles, the memory of former scenes
of delight and despair which they have enacted—these
and other associations enable Goethe to voice his
changing emotion at a pitch of saturation which we do
not look for in pure monologue. Here and everywhere

in the poem Goethe justifies his use of his dramatic
figures by the wealth of self-expression which he succeeds
in extracting from himself with their assistance. We
have only to put this passage beside the corresponding
passage in *Hamlet*—Hamlet's cursing and reaction from
cursing in a typical bit of Shakespearean monologue
—to see that this Goethean way of writing, inconsistent
as it may seem in jog-trot places, abundantly justifies
itself when the crucial moment comes:

> For it cannot be
> But I am pigeon-liver'd and lack gall
> To make oppression bitter, or ere this
> I should have fatted all the region kites
> With this slave's offal: bloody, bawdy villain!
> Remorseless, treacherous, lecherous, kindless villain!
> O, vengeance!
> Why, what an ass am I! This is most brave,
> That I, the son of a dear father murder'd,
> Prompted to my revenge by heaven and hell,
> Must, like a whore, unpack my heart with words,
> And fall a-cursing, like a very drab,
> A scullion!
> Fie upon 't! foh! About, my brain!

There can be no absolute comparison between this
passage and the passage from *Faust*; they belong to
different worlds, and they serve different purposes.
But there remains a curiously suggestive point of
contact. Hamlet rounds the same emotional corner as
Faust, there is a moment when we can feel his mind
flowing in Faust's channel, but he has nothing of the
Faustian opportunity to probe and elucidate the
moment or to draw us into it.

Take any of the typical passages in *Faust* and the
same analysis can be made—the suicide scene where the
angels' song breaks in with precisely the same inwardness
as the spirits' song here; the close of the Helena episode
with its symphonic voices; the dying moments of Faust.
In all these passages we can recognize a way of poetry

which is consummate in its kind. There is no uneasy compromise, as there sometimes is in *Torquato Tasso*, between the requirements of the drama and the lyrical demands made upon it. Clearly the Faust legend lends itself with far greater advantage to Goethe's purpose. And it is easy to discover where the advantage lies. It is the supernatural character of the scenes which makes them so amenable. When we reflect on it, we can quickly see that the supernatural agencies of the poem must operate in Goethe's way on the freedom of the persons in it; just like the Goethean lyricism they make for an overruling of the individual voices and a subordinating of them to some mysteriously enclosing life. By subduing the common reality to an unseen world they diminish the separateness of the characters just as Goethe does when he speaks through them instead of letting them speak for themselves.

Thus the Faust legend meets the poet half-way. The spectral qualities which the persons in the Faust legend bring with them as figures in a ghost-story accord perfectly with the kind of unreality with which Goethe invests them when he makes them mouthpieces of himself. What his lyrical mood does to the characters when he takes them over is anticipated by the supernatural forces which have presided over them from the beginning. And so Goethe is enabled by the very aura and atmosphere of the legend to put himself completely behind it, and to make the whole poem the voice of himself.

But a difficulty remains. Granting that this way of reading *Faust* is sound enough for large areas of the text, what is to be done with the more realistic and more dramatic of the early scenes and, above all, with the Gretchen tragedy, so direct, so human, so intelligible? For after all that has been said about lyrical origins, the Gretchen tragedy invites offhand a straightforward dramatic reading and usually gets it. There seems to be no urgent call for a subtler reading of it, nor is it readily apparent that any subtler reading of it is possible, so why not take this part of the poem as it stands, enjoy it for what it seems to be—as clean a piece of tragic drama as could be desired—and let the rest of the poem look after itself?

The answer must be that when we read the Gretchen tragedy in this spirit we are not seeing it as Goethe saw it when he allowed it to subside into the longer sequence of scenes which constitutes the complete *Faust*. It would be absurd to say flatly that it should not be read as simple tragedy. This is probably how every one first reads it, it is an almost necessary stage in the appreciation of it. But it is not absurd to say that if we continue to read it exclusively in this spirit—as if it were a pure love-drama, a German successor to *Romeo and Juliet*, and this only—we are not reading it in its poetic entirety, we are not entering into all its finer values. We have already noted that the figures in the Gretchen tragedy, sharply drawn as they are, do not possess the individuality of Shakespeare's figures; the long native tradition seems too strong in them for that. Moreover, they do not seem to enjoy the kind of continuous vitality proper to drama. So long as they are immediately before us they are alive and real, but once they withdraw from the scene they forfeit their reality and vanish into thin air. They have nothing of the continuity of Ibsen's figures, whose life-history before or after the play seems as vivid as their life on the stage; they are not even particularized enough to allow us to reconstruct them in any off-stage scenes whatsoever. We do not ask about the early life of Gretchen, or what Faust would have done if he had not met Mephistopheles. All this is quite incongruous here. These characters have an eerie knack of appearing and disappearing, partly suggested by the magical associations of the poem, but due also to its texture, its swift changefulness, its

readiness to break into song and ballad, and, most
of all, we must surmise, to Goethe's way of conceiving his characters, his lyrical concentration on
them at the moment of using them, his indifference
to them when they were not serving his passionate
purpose.

This will be readily conceded for Mephistopheles who
is supernatural by legendary right, being either the
devil or some sort of devil and quite without pedigree.
But it is true also of Faust. There is nothing more
unconvincing in the whole poem than the unnecessary
excursion into Faust's past life when he tells Wagner
about his father's activities, the truth of the matter
being that to have had a father is as superfluous for him
as it is necessary for Hamlet. His past is too vague,
too unreal, to admit even of this slight elaboration.
Like Mephistopheles he is only there when he is wanted.
And so with the others. They live with great intensity
in all that they say and do at the moment, but the
affiliations, the before and after of strictly dramatic
life, scarcely pertain to them. However real they seem
at first, they all prove to be ghosts when we apply this
simple test. Even these Gretchen scenes, we find, are
in their degree spectral and, if we read them rightly, we
can pass from them to the phantasmagoria of the Second
Part without incongruity. The quality of the scene
in which Helena disappears magically for ever, or of the
scene in which the four grey spectre-women gather at
the door of the aged Faust, is present, faintly present,
even in Frau Marthe's garden or in Gretchen's bedroom.
The shudder which Gretchen feels when she enters her
room after Faust and Mephistopheles have been there
is, as it were, the shudder of apprehensiveness, the sense
of other and supra-individual forces which plays about
the whole poem. When she reproaches Faust for
keeping company with Mephistopheles and confesses
that if Mephistopheles is with them she cannot care for

him: "This disturbs me so that when he comes and joins us I feel as if I had ceased to love you":

> Das übermannt mich so sehr,
> Dass, wo er nur mag zu uns treten,
> Mein' ich sogar, ich liebte dich nicht mehr,

she is vaguely sensing, and enabling us to sense, the mysterious link which makes these two figures into one. Here, as sometimes in *Torquato Tasso*, the lyrical psychology breaks with a subtle beauty through the dramatic.

But if this interpreting of overtones is brushed aside as too elusive, there is a more drastic argument. Why, if Goethe meant the Gretchen tragedy to be read as drama, did he insert the Walpurgisnacht in the middle of it? The circumstance that he wrote it more than twenty years later than the adjacent scenes does not alter the fact that he placed it where he did. It may serve to remind us that he must have placed it there very deliberately. Coming as it does in the thick of the tragedy it has not always been welcomed, and few have accepted it heartily; whether as narrative interlude or dramatic it cannot pass unquestioned. The native explanation of it, which we have already touched upon, gives a quite adequate reason for Goethe's writing it and inserting it somewhere in the text prior to the opening of the Second Part, but it does little to explain why he inserted it here. Why did he not pool it with the Witch's Kitchen and get it over early, or else defer it till the tragedy was ended? It is not easy to be satisfied with the view that Goethe inserted it where he did in order to indicate the lapse of time, because at nearly every other point *Faust* is independent of any time-illusion, and we can only ask: "Why not at this point?" Nor is it satisfactory to say that the Walpurgisnacht is a picture of Faust's attempt to distract and deaden himself since, at the crucial moment in

Gretchen's life, this cannot interest us sufficiently to justify the interruption of her tragedy; while his remorse —which does interest us—is powerfully expressed in other scenes and barely indicated here. Mephistopheles, of course, is trying to drag Faust yet more deeply in the mire, but this could have been illustrated later and nothing would be lost. If Faust's lurid distractions are introduced as a parallel or companion piece to Gretchen's misery, why make the attempt, why split a magnificent tragedy in two? Poetically the Walpurgisnacht still abides our question. Calvin Thomas, an able commentator, went so far as to say that there was no explanation which was altogether creditable to Goethe.

This is the *impasse* we come to if we insist on reading *Faust* and the Walpurgisnacht in terms of action and character. If, on the other hand, we shift to a more inward reading, considering the movement of the Gretchen tragedy into the Walpurgisnacht and out again as a sequence of moods comparable to that through which the poem passes in the scene of Faust's curse, but on a more elaborate and more protracted scale, the problem solves itself. One reading and one only is now possible. The Gretchen tragedy with its powerful lyrical undercurrents can pass emotionally into the Walpurgisnacht by creating it under extreme stress as an escape, a visionary or supernatural or mythical escape, from the torture which it is enacting and suffering. This or something closely akin to it is the satisfactory reading which Calvin Thomas missed.

There is everything in the content of the Walpurgisnacht to suggest this reading. It is clearly the myth, the darkly created folk-myth, belonging to Gretchen's world, and we need not doubt that Goethe saw it so. We have only to remember the short poem, "Die erste Walpurgisnacht," in which Goethe, anticipating an idea which Heine popularized, suggests how the Germanic mythology was converted into a Walpurgisnacht by the impact of Christianity on it.   But there is no need to go outside of *Faust*.   There is evidence enough of Goethe's conception of the Walpurgisnacht in the way he dealt with the scenes that precede and follow it.   He first printed the Gretchen tragedy in the Fragment of 1790. But instead of printing the whole of it from his manuscript of the *Urfaust* he stopped enigmatically at the cathedral scene, in which Gretchen swoons away in anguish.   That is to say, he stopped at the scene which in the completed First Part is immediately followed by the Walpurgisnacht, as if realizing at this comparatively early date that something important had yet to be written and inserted here before he could allow himself to proceed with the publication of the rest of the tragedy. No slighter consideration could justify the violent dismemberment of his text.   Who can believe that Goethe was merely actuated by the thought that the prison scene only existed as yet in prose, and that he would withhold it in the hope of versifying it, as he ultimately did?   This is too slender a reason.   The Walpurgisnacht or something like it must have been already in his mind as a sufficiently vital element in his conception of this part of the work to prevent his printing the whole of the Gretchen tragedy without it.

The completed First Part gives a surer clue.   What Goethe does here is to lift the woodland cavern scene, Wald und Höhle, from the place which it occupied in the Fragment to an earlier and less suitable place before the seduction of Gretchen.   On dramatic grounds he had no business to do this; the scene belongs where he first put it—after the seduction.   Only the Walpurgisnacht can account for its removal.   To make the Walpurgisnacht plausible, as a passing of the tragedy into vision, a bursting of it, as it were, into its own mythology, he needed as a preparation for it the close progression of native scenes which the Wald und Höhle scene interrupted.   When this scene with its scarcely

Faustian monologue and its far from native note was advanced to an earlier position Goethe was left with just the assortment of folk-scenes which he required; all he had to do was to arrange them in an emotional crescendo. As finally arranged, the sequence is perfect. First, and directly after the seduction, comes the harsh gossip of Lieschen at the well, then Gretchen's agitated prayers before the common shrine, then the luridly conventional disgust of Valentin, and then the hallucinations and the collapse of Gretchen in the crowded cathedral, followed immediately by darkness and the witches' revel. Remembering that the individual minds of this poem are always ready to efface themselves in the interest of the total mind, we cannot but see a cunning suggestiveness in this abrupt transition from Gretchen's loss of consciousness to the nightmare of the Brocken. What can Goethe have meant but that the poem, using Gretchen's swoon to make the transition, shifts from waking to sleeping and dreams its Walpurgisnacht. "It seems," says the text significantly, "that we have entered the sphere of dreams and magic":

> In die Traum- und Zaubersphäre
> Sind wir, scheint es, eingegangen.

In this light the Walpurgisnacht is simply the outcome of a movement in the native emotion of the tragedy which begins with Gretchen's surrender to Faust and with the consequent unsettling of her conscience and culminates at the point where she breaks under the strain and the poem breaks with her. The releasing vision when it comes is not Gretchen's vision, it is the poem's vision, and she is only an instrument in the bringing of it forth. It is not, if we look closely, Gretchen's mind into which we are drawn, it is rather the crowd-mind which she shares with Valentin, Lieschen, and the rest.

The scenes do their best to suggest what they cannot

say outright. Stage by stage the superstitious folk-mind creeps over them. Lieschen begins with her idle rumours; Gretchen follows with her fear of public disgrace; next Valentin puts his curse on her in the open street, speaking with the whole community at his back; then she kneels in the packed cathedral nave, crushed by the censure of her environment, the reverberating music swelling the voice of the world's wrath, till finally the fearful mood of sin, shame, and uncleanliness comes to the breaking-point, Gretchen swoons, and the lewd phantasmagoria begins.

We have to choose. Either Goethe acted wantonly at a critical moment in his great poem, or he—consistently and for these good reasons—subordinated the dramatic to the lyrical, letting the Walpurgisnacht grow out of the mood of the poem, much as one musical theme grows out of another. There is no doubt which of these two explanations is preferable. And when we have said our worst about the capricious Intermezzo, Walpurgisnachtstraum, which follows—it is in one sense appropriate. It lets the larger dream which began with Gretchen's swoon spend itself by getting thinner and thinner, till suddenly it snaps and plunges the poem back into the torture it had escaped. The jump from the close of the Intermezzo—the thinnest and airiest lines in the poem, sung "pianissimo"—to Faust's loud cries of exasperation at Mephistopheles—the only prose scene in the final text—is just what this reading of the Walpurgisnacht calls for. The retention of the prose, here and nowhere else in the poem, is significant; it punctuates the rude awakening as nothing else could.

This arrangement of the Gretchen scenes around the Walpurgisnacht is in direct contrast with the Helena scenes. In his first great adventure with Mephistopheles Faust yields blindly to chance, instinct, desire, whatever is obscure and unintelligent in the life of the mind; he

sees Gretchen in passing and must have her regardless
of any considerations but those of his confused passion;
clouds and darkness settle upon the last scenes of the
tragedy. In the second he recognizes Helena as an
intellectual and spiritual ideal, which he goes in search
of and ultimately touches in an irradiation of light.
This is easy to see. What is less apparent is the close
adjustment of the structure of the poem to this change
of mentality. In the former case the arrangement of
the scenes is only understandable in terms of the subconscious; the Gretchen tragedy draws mysteriously on
the lyricism of Faust's undisciplined passion; the
Walpurgisnacht in its turn grows as a trance or
hallucination out of the Gretchen tragedy. It is a
dream of the lower order, of the emotions—not, like the
Helena episode, a dream of the waking self, consciously
evoked and earned.

Reading *Faust* in this way we lose nothing that is
worth having in the epic and dramatic approach. We
are free as before to get what we can out of the characteri-
zation, the adventures, the panorama, and whatever else
belongs to the work as a story told and a play acted; but
we are relieved of the empty questions, the discrepancies,
the invidiousnesses, which arise on all sides when we
press this point of view farther than Goethe intended
us to press it. We remember that the dramatic life of
the poem is secondary, and that at any moment the
lyrical and musical life may take charge and impose a
logic of its own. We are relieved, for example, of the
moral problem of explaining why Faust after his criminal
desertion of Gretchen is allowed to recuperate on an
upland pasture with nature-elves in attendance, because
it is not just Faust but in a very real sense the poem
which recuperates, with Faust and the elves to make it
vocal. We do not dwell laboriously on the legal aspect
of the compact, because we recognize that the compact
is primarily Goethe's device for getting the most out of

the scenes in which it is used and is not carefully remembered by him as the poem proceeds. The compact enables Faust to express his Titanic idealism as nothing else could, and this is its chief value. Mephistopheles, for that matter, has already made his compact in heaven and has no need of this further one with Faust; it is Faust who forces it on him. Having used the compact to extract a fuller expression of the Faustian idealism than any yet—using the vivid dramatic crisis and all the associations of the old legend to strengthen and fill it out—Goethe virtually forgets it till he needs it again to perform a similar service at the end. The real connection between these two points in the play is more musical than dramatic; we are reminded rather of the recurrence of a *motif* in symphony or opera than of a dramatic argument proper.

The interpreters of *Faust* continually forget this. When Mr. Santayana says in *Three Philosophical Poets* that he can find no trace of improvement in the character of Faust in the whole Second Part his observation is quite sound; it is the implication which is at fault. Neither Faust nor any of the characters in this work are sufficiently individualized to admit of real development. The distinction that is sometimes drawn between Faust the individual and Faust the representative of humanity is, after all, a crude one; in a more intimate reading Faust is neither of these things, he is an instrument in Goethe's orchestra, an ingredient rather than a whole; and in this capacity it is not fitting that he should undergo moral regeneration or suffer a change of heart. He must go on voicing the invincible aspiration of the human spirit to master the universe, much as the trombone player goes on playing his trombone. He does this from first to last; there is no change, and no change of this sort should be looked for. Goethe is quite frank. Faust strides over Philemon and Baucis almost as ruthlessly as he strode over Gretchen, and

when he enters heaven his egotism is undiminished.
"Already he outgrows us in might of limb":

> Er überwächst uns schon
> An mächtigen Gliedern,

sing the boy-angels who escort him upwards. If there
are sins to commit in heaven he will commit them.
What Mr. Santayana fails to bring out is that the
development is in the poem as a whole, not in its
supposed hero. It is not so much Faust who develops
in wisdom—though he voices the poem's wisdom
whenever it is convenient—it is the poem which develops
in wisdom, and this it does more freely and surprisingly
than any other poem we know.

It is equally mistaken to look for signs of personal
reform in Mephistopheles, as Miss Stawell and Mr.
Dickinson, joint authors of *Goethe and Faust*, seem to do.
It is true that Goethe spoke once of the saving of Mephistopheles—he did not say *reforming*, and he gave him the
freedom of heaven to begin with—and it is true that
in a late scene when Helena vanishes, leaving her robe
in Faust's arms, it is Phorkyas, the Classical metamorphosis of Mephistopheles, who bids him hold it fast,
saying: "It is not the lost goddess, but it is divine":

> Die Göttin ist's nicht mehr, die du verlorst,
> Doch göttlich ist's.

These words are no irony, they are Goethe's wisdom at
a supreme moment. If he lets Mephistopheles say them
it may well be for want of a better spokesman; he could
not give them to the "Chorus," because the light-minded
chorus already in attendance would be grossly inappro-
priate. His chief concern was that the words should
be spoken, and he did not care deeply by whom,
especially at a point of symbolical exaltation in the
poem at which the sense of individual existences all
but disappears.

It follows that the personal hero of traditional epic and drama must not be sought here. When Mr. Lascelles Abercrombie, in *The Idea of Great Poetry*, censures *Faust* for the failure of its central character to hold our interest throughout, he is misapprehending the quality of the work. He is asking it to conform with standards of epic and dramatic poetry which are incompatible with it. It is the same nearly everywhere; the German critics offend as regularly as the English.

CHAPTER VI

THE POSITION OF "FAUST"

WE shall not go far wrong if we associate the writing of the *Urfaust* chiefly with the last phase of Goethe's life in Frankfurt when he was engaged to Lili Schönemann and moving in her showy circle. In a letter to Auguste Stolberg on 17th September, 1775, Goethe says that he wrote a scene of his *Faust* that morning, and while the rest of the evidence is inconclusive, we have strong reasons for thinking that the difference in time of composition between this scene and the bulk of the others cannot be great. Everything points to rapid writing. So far as we know with any certainty Goethe wrote nothing prior to living in Weimar that he did not write quickly. *Götz von Berlichingen, Werther, Clavigo*—the longer and more carefully considered of his other youthful works—were all completed in a few weeks, while shorter works which are nearest to the *Urfaust* in feeling—*Satyros*, for example—are little more than impromptus. The *Urfaust* itself, the only early work about which we are in doubt, has all the marks of speed; probably every scene was written as the scene on 17th September was written—at a sitting, rapidly, in the midst of distractions—for they are all closely allied in character and never seem to have been laboured or overworked, while the Gretchen tragedy, which is by far the larger part of the whole, is scarcely thinkable as a work of piecemeal activity; it must have been written under the stress of a continuous inspiration.

The letters to Auguste Stolberg, his intimate correspondent during these last critical months in Frankfurt,

are more suggestive of the *Urfaust*, and on inner grounds
more likely to be contemporary with the writing of it,
than any others. They are Faust-like as the earlier
letters to Kestner are Werther-like. They show Goethe
leading a sultry distraught existence, shot with sudden onsets of rapture and despair, outwardly drifting
from one social engagement to another, inwardly con-
sumed with a burning fever. "Unhappy fate, that will
not allow me a middle position. Either I clutch and
cling at one point, or I roam to the four winds of heaven"
(Unseeliges Schicksal das mir keinen Mittelzustand
erlauben will. Entweder auf einem Punkt fassend,
festklammernd, oder schweifen gegen alle vier Winde).
This he cries with Faustian turbulence in a letter of
3rd August, and in the letter of 17th September, mentioned above, he compares himself to the rat that,
having taken poison, drinks and eats all it finds yet
cannot quench the deadly flames within, which takes
us to the *Urfaust* again and lets us see that the inimitable
rat-song sung by the roystering students in Auerbach's
Keller, little as we might suspect it on a chance reading,
is personal—a humorous picture of himself in his
amorous entanglement. "It dashed this way and that
and drank from every puddle. It gnawed and scratched
the whole house in its frenzy, yet all to no purpose. So
many an anguished leap it gave, the poor creature soon
had its fill, as if it had love in its belly":

> Sie fuhr herum, sie fuhr heraus
> Und soff aus allen Pfützen,
> Zernagt, zerkratzt das ganze Haus,
> Wollt nichts ihr Wüten nützen.
> Sie thät so manchen Ångstesprung
> Bald hätt das arme Tier genung
> Als hätt es Lieb im Leibe.

All this brings Lili Schönemann much nearer to the
Urfaust than Friederike Brion or the Frankfurt Gretchen.
It was Lili who was consuming him like a poison and

giving him the inspiration and the refrain of his rat-song—"as if he had love in his belly"—or rather it was the dilemma in which she had put him—love, passionate love, pulling him towards her and all his greater ambition pulling him away. This does not mean that Lili was a model for Gretchen; she stood for all that Gretchen was not. She was wealthy, worldly, and not of the people. It means rather that the whole Lili affair must have played about the writing of the *Urfaust* and poured its fever into it.

If we look closely at the Lili songs—especially those written early in the year 1775—we find that they touch the *Urfaust* very closely. Gretchen's spinning-song, beginning with the refrain, "My rest is gone, my heart is heavy, never shall I find my rest again":

> Meine Ruh ist hin,
> Mein Herz ist schwer,
> Ich finde sie nimmer
> Und nimmermehr,

and coming back to it with grinding iteration, has precisely the returning movement, the confinement within a magic circle, stated in the most famous of the Lili songs. "If I wish to withdraw, pull myself together and escape, the next moment I find myself drifting back to her. . . . I have to live now in her magic circle and to her tune":

> Will ich rasch mich ihr entziehen,
> Mich ermannen, ihr entfliehen,
> Führet mich im Augenblick,
> Ach, mein Weg zu ihr zurück.
>
> .   .   .   .
>
> Muss in ihrem Zauberkreise
> Leben nun auf ihre Weise.

The lover of Lili has lost his peace of mind, just as Gretchen has—"Gone your industry and your repose" (Weg dein Fleiss und deine Ruh)—and, like Gretchen again, he is alive to the soundness of the impulse which has entangled him.   "Are you held," he says to himself, "by her youthful bloom, her fair form, her eye so true and kind?"

> Fesselt dich die Jugendblüte,
> Diese liebliche Gestalt,
> Dieser Blick voll Treu und Güte?

while Gretchen says, more poignantly but in the same terms, "All that drove me to it was so kind and dear":

> Doch—alles was mich dazu trieb,
> Gott! war so gut, ach war so lieb.

And why, we may ask, does this lover of Lili in a companion song picture himself, here and nowhere else in a strictly personal lyric, as a simple lad living contentedly in his moonlit chamber and now drawn forth into the social world, unless it be that deep in Goethe's mind the mood of these songs was intertwined with the Gretchen mood and unconsciously borrowed its folk-song note for a moment?   "Why do you irresistibly draw me into all this glitter?   Was I not happy before in the empty night?   There I lay, a simple lad, locked in my little room, with the mysterious moonlight around me":

> Warum ziehst du mich unwiderstehlich,
> Ach, in jene Pracht?
> War ich guter Junge nicht so selig
> In der öden Nacht?
>
> Heimlich in mein Zimmerchen verschlossen,
> Lag im Mondenschein,
> Ganz von seinem Schauerlicht umflossen. . .

The experience Goethe here attributes to himself is closer to Gretchen's experience when she is drawn to Faust than to his own experience when he is drawn to Lili, for though he dislikes Lili's world, as he tells us later in the poem, and is somewhat below her socially, he is not a moonlit rustic and can scarcely have come

directly by this folk-song attitude. It is one more hint
that the Gretchen theme and the Lili theme were active
in his poetic mind at the same time.

This bond between the Lili songs and the *Urfaust*
only serves to give point and vitality to the contrast
between them. For even where we recognize a resemblance, the resemblance is quickly lost in a sense of
difference. Putting the two together, the little group of
Lili poems and the whole of the *Urfaust*, it is hard to
believe that Goethe wrote both at the same time of
life, and perhaps under the same inspiration. In the
tragedy of the *Urfaust* all is desire and pursuit, passionate
wooing, conquest, extremity. "Hear me, you must get
me the girl . . . if the sweet young thing does not lie
in my arms to-night, we part at midnight":

> Hör, du musst mir die Dirne schaffen!
>
> .   .   .   .   .
>
> Wenn nicht das süsse junge Blut
> Heut nacht in meinen Armen ruht,
> So sind wir um Mitternacht geschieden.

These are Faust's words after his first sight of Gretchen,
and the rest is all of a piece. For downright master-
fulness in love-making there is nothing quite like it, not
even in Shakespeare, where we look for what is masterful.
Faust sweeps Gretchen into his power with an assertive-
ness, an absoluteness, which would be melodramatic at
any level of poetic composition short of the highest.
Mephistopheles pleads with him that time is essential,
and even desirable, if the full pleasure is to be extracted,
but Faust says "Away with Time" and Mephistopheles
does his best to comply. Gretchen is decoyed, seduced,
ruined, and abandoned; she is picked up, then cast
aside; Goethe never wavers. Faust has his moments of
remorse, but they have no effect on the issue. Gretchen
faces the agony of the scaffold alone.

And now the Lili songs. Here there is no masculine

initiative; it is the lover who is ensnared, bound hand and foot in the toils that he is powerless to break. He has no active part in it, he is going his inoffensive way when suddenly, unaccountably, he is taken prisoner. In one poem we see him held by an invisible string in the sweetest bondage; in another he is the tame bear in Lili's menagerie, which runs into the farthest corner, only to return and lay its head in her lap; and when it is all over and he has his freedom again, he wears the sign of captivity on his foot. "Like a bird which breaks its string and returns to the woods, he still trails with him a piece of the string, his prison's shame. He is not the freeborn bird that he was, he has belonged to someone":

> Wie ein Vogel, der den Faden bricht
> Und zum Walde kehrt,
> Er schleppt, des Gefängnisses Schmach,
> Noch ein Stückchen des Fadens nach:
> Er ist der alte freigeborne Vogel nicht,
> Er hat schon jemand angehört.

Speaking carelessly, we might take a hint from what has been said and argue that the Lili songs differ from the *Urfaust* as Gretchen from Faust. There is a measure of truth in this, but it is not enough, for Gretchen is quickly drawn into Faust's vortex and lives desperately, while the Lili songs remain within strangely temperate bounds and never reach the accents of passion. They belong to a different kind—a different world—of poetry, and cannot be described in terms of the other world, though they may touch it at moments.

This marks the beginning of an important bifurcation of Goethe's lyricism into Faustian and non-Faustian. From now on his casual lyricism, expressing itself in a loose succession of songs, ballads, and other short poems, consistently preserves the quieter characteristics which distinguish the Lili songs from the Gretchen tragedy, while the Faustian lyricism, less regular in its flow, but drawing on the same inner experiences and operating

continuously on Goethe's mind, works in the bolder
vein of the *Urfaust* and the Faust legend.   If we arrange
the short poems side by side with *Faust*, putting early
with early, middle with middle, and late with late,
and making whatever closer adjustments the immense
Goethe commentary and a patient study of the two texts
help us to make, we have no difficulty in establishing
this general distinction and pursuing it as far as we
choose.

The distinction cannot be clearly established before
about 1775, the date at which we have just drawn it.
Prior to this date Goethe's lyrics are ablaze with energy,
full of anticipations of the mood and the vigour of
Faust.   The exuberance of the Strassburg love-poems
—"My heart beat loud, then quick to horse":

> Es schlug mein Herz: geschwind zu Pferde!

the imperiousness of "Ganymed"—"Up, up I strive;
the clouds float down; they bow to my yearning love":

> Hinauf, hinauf strebt's!
> Es schweben die Wolken
> Abwärts, die Wolken
> Neigen sich der sehnenden Liebe,

and the defiant self-reliance of *Prometheus*—"Here I
sit and make men in my image":

> Hier sitz' ich, forme Menschen
> Nach meinem Bilde,

represent a vein of poetic feeling which is not characteristic of Goethe's short poems as a whole and is very
soon absent from them.   But it is not that the vein runs
dry with the passing of his early youth.   What happens
is that it goes over into *Faust*.   Once the Faust theme
takes hold of Goethe's mind it appropriates all that it
needs for its own purposes, all the dynamic, aggressive,
volitional moods that can be made to accord with it,
and resolutely prevents them from passing into any

non-Faustian forms of expression, even during the long
periods of years when *Faust* is in abeyance and seemingly
out of mind.   Thus the strenuous notes first sounded in
the early odes and songs must be sought after about
1775, exclusively or almost exclusively in the domain
of *Faust*, where we shall find that they never fail to
recur even in the last stages of writing.   Faust's outcry
at his first vision of Helena is as vehement as anything
in the youthful lyrics, it is even more vehement, though
it was probably written in his eightieth year.   "Let
the breath of life leave me if ever I wean myself from
thee.   The fair form that once delighted me in the
magic mirror was a mere bubble beside this beauty.
To thee I now devote my every impulse, my passion's
essence, devotion, love, worship, madness":

> Verschwinde mir des Lebens Atemkraft,
> Wenn ich mich je von dir zurückgewöhne!—
> Die Wohlgestalt, die mich voreinst entzückte,
> In Zauberspiegelung beglückte,
> War nur ein Schaumbild solcher Schöne!—
> Du bist's, der ich die Regung aller Kraft,
> Den Inbegriff der Leidenschaft,
> Dir Neigung, Lieb', Anbetung, Wahnsinn zolle.

His magnificent impatience at the insensate waste of
energy in the ebb and flow of ocean tides, voicing itself
in such colossal half-lines as "And it is possible," or
"The thing displeased me":

> Und es ist möglich! . . .
> Und das verdross mich. . . .

is more Promethean than anything in the early *Prometheus*, and it is of still later date than the outcry to
Helena, belonging almost certainly to the year 1831.
The Faust theme, fastening upon Goethe's mind in the
storm and stress of youthful days, preserves this stormy
vein in him to the end, and liberates it periodically in
great gusts of emotion.

On the other hand, it is only when the Faust legend invades Goethe's creative mind and entrenches itself permanently there that his incidental lyricism—the lyricism of his short poems—begins to find itself and to speak with those accents which make it supreme and unlike all else. This is not to belittle the splendour of the Friederike songs and the Wetzlar and Frankfurt odes, it is merely to recognize that the prevailing accents of this early work are not primarily those which make Goethe's mature lyricism the illustrious thing it is. They are not exclusively his accents, they might have come from another. We can compare these early poems in ardour with Burns and Sappho and recognize that Goethe can hold his own with them in passionate song. Yet it is not because he can do this that we prize him as a writer of short poems, we do not think of him as rivalling or competing with these singers, or with any other "lyric voice" that is "all a wonder and a wild desire"; we do not measure his lyrical genius in terms of passion, tempest, and sudden magic, though there are times when he is with the greatest in this vein; we measure it by other qualities which it is slow to establish, but which, once established, preside over it to the end. They are the qualities which, while in a measure antici-pated by the prose-poem *Werther*—*Faust*, we called it, in a minor key—and by observant lyricism such as "Der Wandrer," do not predominate in the short poems till we come to the Lili songs with their suffering, yielding, palpitating, but watchful and receptive life. They are the qualities displayed—as far as one poem can display what was to lend itself with infinite variety to the modulations of a lifetime—in "Herbstgefühl," another Lili poem of 1775, less famous than the Friederike songs, but more specifically Goethean, more clearly indicative of the kind of poetry of which he was to be the unrivalled master. "Fatten your greenness, O leaves on the vine-trellis, climbing here at my window. And

you, twin-berries, fill out and ripen to a glossier plump-
ness. The parting gaze of the mother-sun nurtures
you; the fruitful fullness of the heavens rustles about
you; the breath of the magic, friendly moon cools you;
and, watering you, from these my eyes, lo! the swelling
tears of ever-reviving love":

> Fetter grüne, du Laub,
> Am Rebengeländer
> Hier mein Fenster herauf!
> Gedrängter quellet,
> Zwillingsbeeren, und reifet
> Schneller und glänzend voller!
> Euch brütet der Mutter Sonne
> Scheideblick; euch umsäuselt
> Des holden Himmels
> Fruchtende Fülle;
> Euch kühlet des Mondes
> Freundlicher Zauberhauch,
> Und euch betauen, ach!
> Aus diesen Augen
> Der ewig belebenden Liebe
> Vollschwellende Tränen.

This is not the poetry of the Strassburg days, but in its
different way it holds its own with it. Has any poet
before or since succeeded as Goethe succeeds here in
letting his lover's tears merge into the process of nature
and become one with the sunlight, and the moonlight,
and the healing dews of autumn? There is nothing
attenuated, the poem is as ripe and full as the grape-
vines which it immortalizes. The withholding of certain
lyrical elements, present in the earlier poems, far from
depreciating the vitality of what is left, has liberated
something which is all the richer for being free to move
and expand by itself. The virtues of this poem, as of
all the Lili poems, are the opposite of those that prevail
in *Faust*; they come from watching and waiting, from
submission, from reserve, from understatement, while
Faust draws on the poetry of divine impatience, self-
assertion, and excess. Yet the poems are serene and

consummate in their kind, co-equal with *Faust*, not subordinate to it.

"Herbstgefühl" is not a key poem; it is a good example from the year 1775, but almost any other poem of this or of later date would serve. We shall not find any other with the same slowly bursting mellowness, or with the same drooping grape-cluster of words; each poem has its new moment of life, there is no borrowing; but all the poems are alike in this—they do not address us as paralipomena to *Faust* but move serenely in their unassailable non-Faustian world. As it happened, the years that followed 1775 were those in which the Faust impulse in Goethe was at its quietest, and this circumstance, due in large measure, if not wholly, to the personal dominion over him of Charlotte von Stein, gave the other side of his poetic nature every opportunity to develop and to consolidate what it had gained in writing the Lili songs. It is perhaps in this period, the Charlotte period, that Goethe's quieter habit of lyrical self-expression took its deep hold and became inalienably part of him. These are the years of the poems to Charlotte, the least Faustian, the most gently submissive of all; the best of the Mignon poems, smouldering with the indignation of exile, yet never bursting into flame and open revolt; the seductive ballads of the fisherman and of the erlking, all magical with the thrill and the terror of a mysterious passivity; melodious lyrics breathing peace, the loss of peace, the desire for peace; gravely reflective odes celebrating the boundaries of a mortal life that is noble beside the beasts, but puny beside the gods—it matters not where we go in this period, we find the non-Faustian vein in the ascendant, and reaching what we can now see to be its farthest extreme of differentiation in the feminine and subtly transcendental dramas of *Iphigenie auf Tauris* and *Torquato Tasso*. Even where a Faustian note is sounded it quickly changes to one less masterful. "Rastlose

Liebe" illustrates this. It opens with six agitated and
tempestuously careering lines that Faust might have
spoken, lines that recall the wilder poetry of the Frankfurt period, such as "Wanderers Sturmlied," sung
almost incoherently in the teeth of the hailstorm.
"Into the snow and the rain and the wind, through
fogs and mists in the steaming chasms, on and on,
without rest!

> Dem Schnee, dem Regen,
> Dem Wind entgegen,
> Im Dampf der Klüfte,
> Durch Nebeldüfte,
> Immer zu! Immer zu!
> Ohne Rast und Ruh!

And then, with an instinctive change of metre into slower
falling rhythms, the poem relaxes and half withdraws;
the storms of love are more painful than the storms of
sorrow, yet there is no escape from them, they are the
glory as they are the anguish of living, they must be
accepted and understood. "I would sooner fight my
way through suffering than endure so many joys of life.
All this drawing of heart to heart, ah! how strangely it
fashions pain. What, shall I flee, flee to the woods?
'Twere all in vain. Crown of life, joy without repose,
love 'tis thou":

> Lieber durch Leiden
> Möcht' ich mich schlagen,
> Als so viel Freuden
> Des Lebens ertragen.
> Alle das Neigen
> Von Herzen zu Herzen,
> Ach, wie so eigen
> Schaffet das Schmerzen!
>
> Wie, soll ich fliehen?
> Wälderwärts ziehen?
> Alles vergebens!
> Krone des Lebens,
> Glück ohne Ruh,
> Liebe, bist du!

And if in the reflective poem "Ilmenau" he strikes more resonantly Faustian chords and speaks of one whose passion it is to err and to live a life of restless extremes and hazards, he is not speaking of himself, but of his patron, Karl August, his own role being that of the saddened mentor perplexed by his Faustian companion.

We now begin to see *Faust* in its true position in Goethe's poetic universe. It is not, like *Paradise Lost* or *De Rerum Natura* or the *Divine Comedy*, the central and representative poem of a lifetime, it is only half-representative. It comprises one of the two distinct and complementary poetic modes in which Goethe's life-experience is chiefly recorded, and we do not know him as a poet until we have taken due account of both, patiently using the one to supplement or elucidate or correct the other, and indefinitely deferring all questions of priority. The failure of eminent critics to recognize this co-equality of Goethe's non-Faustian poetry with his *Faust* has done much to obscure him. Mr. Santayana's essay on *Faust* is a distinguished case in point; he sees deeply, but makes the serious mistake of suggesting, if only by the plan of his volume, that the poem contains all the data required for the understanding of its author, with the result that he does better justice to *Faust* than to Goethe. We can say the same of Miss Stawell and Mr. Dickinson; when they introduce Goethe as the most imperfect of great poets they can only mean that *Faust* is the most imperfect of great poems—a judgment that few will contest. If on the other hand they had kept Goethe's incomparable shorter lyricism in mind they might as easily have claimed that he is of all poets the least imperfect.

Perhaps it is in the central period of Goethe's life, the period which opens with his journey to Italy and culminates in the all-round Hellenism of his middle years, which offers the best opportunity for comparing the two modes and assessing their respective advantages

the wide plains of earth and ocean.   Others have caught
the physical splendour of Homer's world and will catch
it again.   What distinguishes Goethe is that he masters
the Homeric view of life, showing himself as keenly
alive to the meaning of Zeus as to the meaning of
Achilles, and as deeply imbued with the philosophy
of the Iliad as with its scene and plot.   Goethe's words
in this poem on fate, hope, war, fame, death, and
insecurity, are as fundamental and as authentic as
anything in his other writings; they reach our ears with
a full voice speaking in accents that are natural to it,
yet they are the accents of Homer, and they come
ringing out of Homer's world.   The speech of Pallas
Athene, spoken by her in the disguise of Antilochus to
Achilles, wipes all thought of derivation and literary
experiment from our minds; it is as worthy of Homer as
it is of Goethe.   "Thou hast chosen a precious thing.
Who leaves the earth while he is young walks for ever
young in Persephone's kingdom.   For ever young he
seems to them that follow, for ever desired.   When my
father dies, the aged Nestor, who shall weep for him?
Even from the eyes of his son the gentle tears shall
scarcely fall.   There the old man will lie in his consummation, a glorious example for mankind.   But the young
man, when he falls, awakens an infinite yearning in all
them that come after ":

> Köstliches hast du erwählt.   Wer jung die Erde verlassen,
> Wandelt auch ewig jung im Reiche Persephoneias,
> Ewig erscheint er jung den Künftigen, ewig ersehnet.
> Stirbt mein Vater dereinst, der graue reisige Nestor,
> Wer beklagt ihn alsdann? und selbst von dem Auge des Sohnes
> Wälzet die Träne sich kaum, die gelinde.   Völlig vollendet
> Liegt der ruhende Greis, der Sterblichen herrliches Muster.
> Aber der Jüngling fallend erregt unendliche Sehnsucht
> Allen Künftigen auf. . . .

This is an achievement which not only rivals the
Helena, but in some respects scores over it.   What

mars the perfection of the Helena is the complexity of means by which it is obtained. There is something in the very elaborateness of the carnival and the Classical underworld, the homunculus, the earthquake, the tripod, the mystic mothers, the procession of Galatea, and what not, that conflicts with the lucid, simple, austere Helena who finally addresses us. The Faustian hocus-pocus dogs her all the way. And, if she escapes it for a brief space, it quickly reclaims her. No sooner have we seen and heard her as she is in herself than she is involved in a new set of complications—the magic flight to the North, the union with Faust, the birth and death of Euphorion—all brilliantly symbolizing the absorption of the Classical spirit into the modern world, yet too intricate and mystifying to delight us as Helena delighted us. Why all this palaver?

The answer is simple. Goethe is telling the whole story of his Classicism, the winning and losing of it not less than the possession, and he uses the means appropriate to the poem; the episode is part of *Faust*, and it cannot escape the consequences. We recognize this, we admire the achievement, yet we wish at times that it could have been otherwise, and that this evocation of Hellenism could have been reached in some simpler way more in keeping with the Hellenic spirit.

When this mood is on us we would do well to read the *Achilleis*, where the evocation is not less complete, and where the means are simple and direct. After the labyrinths and the subterranean approaches to Helena here is an open door to Achilles. All Goethe does here is to state his love for Homer in the way that comes most natural to him as a poet—creatively. Subordinating himself to the mind and the fashion of the Homeric poems, he takes up the Iliad where Homer left off and carries it a stage forward, far enough to show how well he has learned, but never straining or over-reaching himself, never forgetting who is master and who is pupil.

This is not a description of the poem, but it conveys the spirit of it, which is instinct with a fine self-surrender and devoid of all vain emulation. By its very closeness to Homer the poem attests its discipleship; and when it succeeds it is as a disciple succeeds who reverently follows his master and is rewarded by the gift, the passing gift, of his master's spirit. Here again the *Achilleis* is truer to its theme than the Helena; the Greek spirit is not hunted and run to earth, but it comes quietly and easily.

The rest of the shorter Classical poems accord with the *Achilleis* in attitude. If we read them closely we find that it is not as a Faustian conqueror that Goethe enters the Classical world. The earliest of his pagan love-poems—the real beginning of his Classicism—have more in them of contemplation and delay than of insistence. Here he is the lover who resists—"Cupido"— or waits—"Morgenklagen"— or accepts—"Der Becher." And in all this he is more Greek, closer to the anthologists and the amorists, than the Faust who thrusts clumsily forward to embrace the Helena he has evoked. In "Der Besuch" the poet finds his beloved sleeping and does not disturb her; he observes her a while and tiptoes away. "Happy I sat, contemplation mysteriously checked the desire to awaken her":

> Freudig sass ich da, und die Betrachtung
> Hielte die Begierde, sie zu wecken,
> Mit geheimen Banden fest und fester.

And if in the *Roman Elegies* which follow he speaks with a full sense of possession—he is now in the midst of the Classical world, mind and senses are proudly saturated with it—even here his spirit is temperate and receptive; it is the great past that speaks while the poet listens and absorbs. "Tell me, O stones! Speak, you high palaces!"

> Saget, Steine, mir an, o sprecht, ihr hohen Paläste!

And again: "This Classic soil delights and inspires me, past and present speak with a louder spell":

> Froh empfind' ich mich nun auf klassischem Boden begeistert;
> Vor- und Mitwelt spricht lauter und reizender mir.

Passages like these, with their pride and their sonority, may serve to remind us that, *Faust* or no, it is always the same poet speaking, and that the weight and energy of his genius is never lacking. The one mode, we shall find, is always latent in the other, putting a reserve of strength behind the quietude or of delicacy behind the passion. If it is true that Goethe never shouts, it is equally true that he never whimpers; never does his passivity become frail, or his defiance noisy; he is as free from stridency in his moments of conquest as he is from repining in his moments of surrender.

Yet the antithesis remains, and *Faust* is *Faust* to the last. If the non-Faustian note ever comes to the fore in it, it is either extraneous—there is a clear instance of this in the Wald und Höhle monologue—or it is quickly subordinated as the action strides mightily forward. The scene at the beginning of the Second Part in which Faust observes the waterfall and the rainbow and recognizes that the absolute is beyond him, "Let the sun be at my back—Life is in the coloured reflex":

> So bleibe denn die Sonne mir im Rücken!
>
> . . . . .
>
> Am farbigen Abglanz haben wir das Leben,

is one of the glories of the poem, but it does little to curb it. It is not long before Faust is pursuing a new ambition, less desperate than the old one, but so vast and arduous that his promise of self-restraint is hardly remembered. Indeed he forgets it himself, for he says later to Mephistopheles in the scene of the Mothers, "In this Nothing of yours I hope to find the Everything":

> In deinem Nichts hoff' ich das All zu finden.

And it is the same in Act V. No sooner has he announced at the age of one hundred that it is time to leave the hereafter alone and be content with the horizon of earth: "The earth is not mute to the man of solid virtue. Why should he go roaming into eternity?"

> Dem Tüchtigen ist diese Welt nicht stumm.
> Was braucht er in die Ewigkeit zu schweifen!

than he sweeps beyond this horizon and enters an incommensurable future.

It is only at the very last, when the poem is surging upwards from earth to heaven, that there is any hint of a deeper reconciliation. The poem tells us here that only if the grace of God is added to the human striving can there be any hope of full salvation. "And if Love is bestowed on him from above, the heavenly host will welcome him":

> Und hat an ihm die Liebe gar
> Von oben teilgenommen,
> Begegnet ihm die selige Schar
> Mit herzlichem Willkommen.

And it is this that Goethe must mean when he speaks in the final stanza of the Eternal-Womanly (das Ewig-Weibliche). He is thinking of that which must be given, and without which the striving is of no avail. But we cannot honestly say that this deep wisdom grows out of the poem; it grows rather out of the other side of Goethe's mind which *Faust* is incapable of expressing. If we wish to understand what das Ewig-Weibliche and the attitude of acceptance meant to him, we have to go outside *Faust* and read the rest of his poetry, and read it long. It is as if at the eleventh hour *Faust* was trying to capitalize what it had not earned or mastered. We can imagine that it is on its way to mastering it, and does ultimately master it though we cannot follow it farther —the poem seems to pass beyond our reach and hearing rather than to stop. All we know when we part from it is that it has not mastered it yet, and that it remains Faustian to the last.   Faust is rejuvenated at the brink of heaven as he had been rejuvenated in the Witch's Kitchen and on his Alpine pasture, and he is ready now to pursue the soul of Gretchen which lures him from above. The atmosphere has changed to rarer and purer, but there is no change in temper.

CHAPTER VII

THE CREATIVE ACT

THERE is no doubt which of the two modes, the Faustian and the non-Faustian, proved more congenial. For Goethe the "first and most genuine" of all forms of poetry was the "occasional" poem, the Gelegenheitsgedicht; by which he did not imply the poetry of formal occasions, but of informal. To be sure, he could write *vers de circonstance* when they were needed—birthday lines, a commemorative play, or a court libretto. But this is not what he meant. He meant the poetry that came when the private occasion, the inward occasion, called for it; he meant the poetry of direct inspiration. And as the direct inspiration is usually brief, he meant in the first place the short poem, the lyrical poem, as he himself understood and practised it.

This is not a narrow definition. It includes poems as different as "Mailied," a larklike trilling of song; "Metamorphose der Pflanzen," an exposition of plant-life; "Amyntas," a parable of domestic renunciation; "Meeresstille," a grandiose sea-picture; "Der Zauber-lehrling," a humorous anecdote; and many others—love lyrics, epigrams, drinking-songs, riddles, hymns, inscriptions, epistles, sonnets, odes, ballads, idylls, in astounding variety. It would be as easy to name fifty poems as to name five, all different, yet all prompted by the usually inconspicuous occasion, all owing their existence to some fitness of time and place, some ripening of experience, some convergence of impulses, and all coming readily to his pen. If we are reminded of Edgar Allan Poe's contention, that the only genuine poems are short poems and that a long poem is a contradiction in terms, we must hasten to distinguish. Poe, a self-conscious and calculating artist, is thinking of the effect of the completed work; he makes the emotional response of some ideal reader the test of a poem's unity; while Goethe, we can be certain, was thinking solely of the creative act, its use and misuse, its comforts and discomforts. His preference, as a maker of poetry, was for poetry which came of itself without much deliberation. And this not from indolence, but from conviction. It was his settled belief that the creative life requires a liberal measure of unconsciousness if it is to thrive. He says in a memorable epigram: "All our endeavour only succeeds at the unconscious moment. How should the rose bloom, if it knew the sun's splendour?"

> All unser redlichstes Bemühn
> Glückt nur im unbewussten Momente.
> Wie möchte denn die Rose blühn,
> Wenn sie der Sonne Herrlichkeit erkennte!

And in his *Geschichte der Farbenlehre* he speaks of the arts in general as something which man continually produces without willing it (ohne zu wollen). Putting these and similar pronouncements beside what we can learn of his poetic life—his waiting upon impulsion, his reticence about the actual writing, his amateurishness on certain technical points—we can satisfy ourselves that when he spoke of occasional poetry he was thinking not least of this inner desideratum.

In this wider sense we may include as occasional poetry whatever poetry came from him freely, all his inspired fragments and first drafts of longer poems, as well as the general run of shorter poems. The line must be drawn at poems which were projected or outlined before he was ready to write them, or at the point where some draft or fragment was taken up again after the first impulse was spent. What Goethe shrank from was the bending of his poetic genius to any task-work, unless he could do it lightly to meet a social need and amuse his friends. As soon as the poem which he had begun detached itself from him, confronted him with its requirements, thrust an explicit problem before him, he was at a disadvantage and knew it. This shows clearly in the notorious difficulty he experienced in completing any longer poems that had lost their momentum in process, and it shows still more clearly in the longer poems that he failed to complete.

Before 1775 all was plain sailing. He wrote what he was impelled to write on the spur of the moment, and he wrote little else; if that left him with an unfinished poem on his hands he was not perturbed, he let it lie. *Götz von Berlichingen* and *Werther* seem to have come almost as easily as his snatches of song; even the *Urfaust* must be regarded as an occasional poem, or a close series of occasional poems, rather than as a project thoughtfully planned and undertaken.

It is only when he puts his youth behind him and his life is growing in seriousness and purpose, that he encounters the problem, so unwelcome to him, of dealing with poetry that is not occasional. He now finds himself less able than of yore to leave his fragments alone; his growing deliberateness of life knocks at the door of his poetic sanctuary, guard it as he may, and tells him that there are works of his which he must finish. And in this spirit, not so much from poetic choice as from moral necessity, he does here and there complete a work the occasion for which lies far behind him in the cold past. *Egmont, Iphigenie auf Tauris, Torquato Tasso*, all of them spontaneous enough in their beginnings, were the reverse of spontaneous in their later stages. Goethe had outlived them; it was useless to wait any longer upon occasion, for the occasion would never come. These were works which had to be finished by an act of will, helped no doubt by his undertakings to his publisher, but helped also by his reluctance to leave them in their rough or fragmentary state. Whatever the reason, he found it advisable to round them off. Yet his heart was all the time with the occasional poem. It was in the years when this new situation first began to dawn on him that he wrote his ballad of the minstrel who protests that he sings "like a bird on the bough":

> Ich singe wie der Vogel singt,
> Der in den Zweigen wohnet.

This, we may take it, is Goethe asserting his determination to guard his poetic life against encroachment, private or official; as far as may be he will write poetry when he desires to write it, and only then. And this, on the whole, is what he did. Neither financial considerations, nor the demands of his fellow-men, nor personal ambition, nor any literary adventuring ever weaned him successfully from his initial position as the occasional and essentially unbusinesslike, unmethodical poet. For one long poem which he completed there were two which he failed to complete; the fragments of middle and later life are not less conspicuous than the early fragments, as *Die Geheimnisse* and *Pandora* testify; year after year he would write little or nothing; in old age he waited upon occasion as he had waited in his youth.

There was only one poem that managed to hold him under longer contract, and that was *Faust*, which he could neither bring himself to leave as a fragment, nor be rid of in one drastic reckoning. Something there was in this Faust theme that would not let him go, and if he was minded to abandon it there was Schiller or Eckermann at his elbow bidding him continue, so that what with one thing and another the poem clung to him, and he to the poem. And thus by a strange irony the poet, who of all great poets was the least willing and the least able to put himself in harness, wore the harness of *Faust* for over fifty years and learned all there was to learn about the kind of poetry he did not instinctively choose to write—the poetry of intention and resolve and conscious mastery.

It is this which gives the Prelude to *Faust* (Vorspiel auf dem Theater) its intimate bearing on the poem. Ostensibly the Prelude deals with the relation of poet to public. The director of a small theatre is short of a play—how he comes to be in this quandary we do not know—and he calls on the poet, his employee, to supply one on short notice. The poet objects and tells him that this is rank prostitution, but he is overruled, it appears, and does his best. On the face of it this is Goethe apologizing for the popular elements in his drama, telling us that it is not thus that he would choose to write, and asking us to bear with him. But this interpretation does not take us very far. When the Prelude was written in the late nineties *Faust* was no longer a work of popular character; most of the simpler scenes, the folk-scenes, had been done more than twenty years before, and the scenes that occupied him in this middle period were among the profoundest and most esoteric that he ever wrote—the compact scene and the Helena, for example. Of course, the Faust theme was, and remained, a folk-theme, lifted out of puppet-plays and chap-books; its traditional tomfoolery clung to it throughout, as Goethe knew too well; but this does not alter the fact that at the time of writing the Prelude he was as far from compromising his art as he had ever been.

The deeper issue in the Prelude is not between poet and public, but between two sides of Goethe's poetic mind—the instinctive and the deliberate. He is at his old trick of self-dramatization, the director in him is telling the poet in him that he must not wait upon occasion, but must resolutely face the task before him —the task of completing a work which, twist and tarry as he may, will impose its inexorable conditions on him and tax his conscious powers to the utmost. "What is the use of talking so much about being in the mood? The mood never comes to those who hesitate. If you pretend to be poets, command your poetry":

> Was hilft es, viel von Stimmung reden?
> Dem Zaudernden erscheint sie nie.
> Gebt ihr euch einmal für Poeten,
> So kommandiert die Poesie!

What the Prelude says is that *Faust* is a poem which deep in his poetic heart Goethe did not wish to complete; and in the Dedication (Zueignung) which precedes it —it was written at about the same time—we see him in doubt. The dream-figures of the poem come hovering before him and he hesitates; they press upon him, and he accepts them. Yet it is rather for the memories they bring with them from *Urfaust* days than for their own sakes that he does so. It is the thoughts of "auld lang syne" that win him over, as they win over Faust at the moment of suicide—another scene, by the way, from the same middle period. When Goethe says that he is seized by "a long unfelt desire for that solemn spirit-world":

> Und mich ergreift ein längst entwöhntes Sehnen
> Nach jenem stillen, ernsten Geisterreich,

he seems to be looking, somewhat illogically, at the past instead of the poem, and to be thinking of Merck and Lili and "the old familiar faces," rather than of the strange new poetic forms that were to be.

It does not follow that the poem is the loser by this lurking incompatibility; it both loses and gains. Where it suffers most is where most long poems suffer—in those transitional passages which have to be supplied between the great climaxes or moments of high inspiration. What Milton, who was born to write long poems, could not always do must not be expected of Goethe, who was born to write short poems. Considering how little suited he was to the logical management of a plot and a continuous theme, it is amazing how well he succeeds. The Witch's Kitchen, not one of the master-scenes but in no sense inadequate, shows what he could do by way of filling a gap, and the holiday scene (Vor dem Thor) shows it in more notable fashion. On the other hand there are passages, especially in the Second Part, which are less happy. Who does not feel that the conjuring and the astrological jargon at the emperor's court, the bizarre allegories of the carnival, and the phantom manœuvring of the battle-scene are below the great argument, that they lack the driving power and the generosity of the rest?

If we look into it we find that these passages had everything against them. It was not merely that Goethe's aptitude for occasional composition was at an obvious disadvantage here in the always troublesome interludes of a long poem. This was the primary handi-cap which he had to reckon with all the time, excepting only the early days when he dashed off the scenes of his *Urfaust*. Another handicap—setting aside the handicap of advancing years, which again and again he grandly surmounted—was that in the long tussle with this poem he had grown away from it and lost all sympathy with its medieval and superstitious origins. Beginning with his journey to Italy, when he took up his task—not very successfully—for a second time, we can trace his growing antipathy for its incorrigibly Gothic character; and this antipathy, inevitable in one whose mind was now turned steadfastly to other ideals, makes itself felt in the later medieval passages, especially in the more pedestrian of them, where he had to rely on the very spookishness which he had come to detest.

In Faust's words when he enters the witch's kitchen —this scene was written, it is worth noting, in the garden of the Villa Borghese in 1788—"I hate all this supernatural nonsense" (Mir widersteht das tolle

Zauberwesen), and in his impatience with the jugglery in this scene, and in scenes of later date, we can detect Goethe's change of mind, his growing distaste. It was not thus that he had amused himself with magic in Auerbachs Keller where—in the first writing of the scene—Faust himself plays the uproarious trick of knives and noses on the drunken students. This is a mood which does not recur; in the later magic there is no zest, the faint note of exasperation is often heard, and sometimes when the poem slackens it becomes louder and grates on us discordantly. We can feel this in the battle scene, at the carnival, and in many another place. The exasperation which we experience here is Goethe's exasperation, which he has not succeeded in mastering. When, on the other hand, he does master it, he turns it to capital account, first comically, when he makes Mephistopheles—the medieval devil—the butt of the pagan underworld playing ludicrous hide-and-seek with the most nauseating monstrosities of antiquity, and persuading himself the while that this is Hellas, and no better than the Brocken after all. "I thought they would all be strangers here, and alas I find nothing but relatives. It is an old, old story; from Harz to Hellas, cousins all the way!"

> Hier dacht ich lauter Unbekannte
> Und finde leider Nahverwandte;
> Es ist ein altes Buch zu blättern:
> Vom Harz bis Hellas immer Vettern!

And again tragically, in the great passage before Faust's death, in which Goethe seems to gather up all that he had come to reject in the character of this strange life-companion of a poem and to put it from him with a final summoning of his strength: "If I could get rid of magic and unlearn my incantations":

> Könnt' ich Magie von meinem Pfad entfernen,
> Die Zaubersprüche ganz und gar verlernen.

There must have been times in the composing of *Faust* when the tension was extreme. Here was a poet whose dominant creative instinct was to relax, to let his poems grow in sleep and in the dark, finding himself compelled to work under deliberate pressure and in the daylight of his waking mind at a poem which he had not so much chosen as saddled himself with, a long poem— he was uneasy when he thought of long poems—and a poem which by early association and by its very character and legend thrust disturbingly before him all that was immature in his former self and gloomily imprisoning in the dark ages of his nation's history. Goethe's long delay in completing the poem was not due to any clear intention of making it cover his lifetime, though in the event this is what it did; it was due to the conflict between his poetic instincts and his poetic labour; his intention was to get the thing finished, and to this end he made elaborate plans and changes of plan, but his nature did not allow him to execute them and compelled him to wait and wait, with the result that while the poem gained at some points by drawing on new experiences and becoming occasional again—the Helena could never have been what it is if he had not first waited to write it, and then waited to finish it—at other points it lost because the tension of writing or the alternative weariness, growing with the years, frustrated or seriously obstructed his natural talents.

But this is not a tale of defeat. It is a tale of hazards and handicaps which in the end do honour to an illustrious achievement. In this extraordinary contest between poet and poem it is the poet who wins. Goethe realized at the end of his life with some surprise that *Faust* had brought him to a new mastery of his art, and that he was at last able to create in himself the divine frenzy of poetry by the operation of his conscious and volitional mind. He speaks of this discovery to Wilhelm von Humboldt in a letter of 1st December, 1831, when

K

Faust was in its very last stages. "Concerning my *Faust* there is much to be said and little. Just at the right moment I remembered the saying: 'If you pretend to be poets, command your poetry':

> Gebt ihr euch einmal für Poeten,
> So kommandiert die Poesie,

and by a secret psychological change (eine geheime psychologische Wendung), which is perhaps worth looking into, I believe that I have risen to a way of writing which, with complete self-consciousness (bei völligem Bewusstsein), has produced something which I can still approve of, though perhaps I shall never be able to swim in this stream again—something that Aristotle and other prose-men would attribute to a sort of madness."

This takes us first and foremost to the concluding scene of *Faust*, written about this time, in which—such now is Goethe's conscious mastery of his art—he draws freely on the imagery of the medieval Church, not because it is near to him and comes instinctively, but because he recognizes in cold blood that this is the imagery which the poem requires. He says to Eckermann on 6th June, 1831: "You will agree that the conclusion where the soul soars upwards was very difficult, and that I might easily have failed in dealing with such elusive and supersensuous things if I had not used the clearly circumscribed forms of the Christian Church to give my poetic intentions the firmness of outline which they needed."

This probably marks the extreme of volitional poetry in all Goethe. It would be difficult to overstate the sophistication which these words imply. Amazingly responsive as Goethe was to the varieties of religious experience, it was only to the less doctrinaire varieties —the pietists and the mystics, Swedenborg, Susanne von Klettenberg, or Filippo Neri—that he felt himself strongly attracted, and all that smacked of ritual or theology was distasteful to him. The "theology too, worse luck" (leider auch Theologie) of fifty years before held good to the last, there can be no question of a change of heart. In electing to use the doctrinal imagery of the Church in the grand finale of *Faust* Goethe was trespassing on a region of high poetry less accessible to him than any he had touched. He had been studying Dante again of late years, but he had studied him with mixed feelings, and it was clear that Dante could never be his poet as Homer and Shakespeare had been. If he now enters Dante's world and temporarily obtains the freedom of it—for that is what it amounts to—it is not by surrendering to it as he had surrendered to Homer, it is by a deliberate fiat of the poetic will, confident now of its sovereign power. And in this spirit, "commanding his poetry" as never before, he rounds off his immense poem with a piece of masterly writing radiant with heavenly beauty and appropriate in every syllable. The fervent imagery of the Pater Ecstaticus, "Eternal torch of joy, burning bond of love, seething pain of heart, foaming delight divine,"

> Ewiger Wonnebrand,
> Glühendes Liebeband,
> Siedender Schmerz der Brust,
> Schäumende Gotteslust,

the vision of the Virgin and the Penitent Women, and the mysticism of the final chorus, all highly ritualistic in flavour, are as authentic as anything in the poem.

If we look for the counterpart of this finale in the shorter verses of his old age we shall find only the briefest and most tentative of lines. Left to himself Goethe is content with the terseness and the reticence of "At night when good spirits are abroad and brush sleep from your brow, and moonbeams and the shimmering stars flood you with the light of eternity, you feel already disembodied and venture to the throne of God":

> Nachts, wann gute Geister schweifen,
> Schlaf dir von der Stirne streifen,
> Mondenlicht und Sternenflimmern
> Dich mit ewigem All umschimmern,
> Scheinst du dir entkörpert schon,
> Wagest dich an Gottes Thron.

This, it seems, is as far as he cared to go in explicit contemplation of the soul's immediate journey into the hereafter, and it was only because he was under contract to the Faust legend that in one august instance he went further and elaborated his intimations into a heavenly ritual. Here, as elsewhere, the spirit of *Faust* forced him beyond the point at which he would have stopped. He was all for understatement, and he had committed himself to a theme which made for overstatement; he preferred to go easy, and the theme put him on his mettle and extended him to the limit, filling his creative mind with its emphasis and dispatch, compelling him, in short, to be a Faustian poet as well as the poet of *Faust*.

This is probably why, when he was not working at *Faust*, he was glad to escape it and recover his happier occasional self. It was not his way to talk much about his poetry; he seldom spoke, perhaps he was seldom able to speak, of what was most intimate in it. But we can see that the poetry which he really cherished and returned to for the pleasure it gave him was poetry of the more spontaneous kind. One of the favourite poems of his late years, as he said more than once, was the little nocturne, "Um Mitternacht," a poem not far removed in theme and mood from the lines just quoted. "At midnight I went, a tiny timid boy, past the churchyard to my father's house, the parsonage; the stars, they shone so fair, so fair, at midnight. When later in life's journey I went to my loved one—she drew me to her, made me go—constellations and northern lights fighting overhead, going and coming I tasted bliss, at midnight. Until at last the full moon's radiance broke so clearly into my darkness, and my mind swiftly, easily musing flung itself about the past and the future, at midnight."

> Um Mitternacht ging ich, nicht eben gerne,
> Klein kleiner Knabe, jenen Kirchhof hin
> Zu Vaters Haus, des Pfarrers; Stern am Sterne,
> Sie leuchteten doch alle gar zu schön;
>   Um Mitternacht.
>
> Wenn ich dann ferner, in des Lebens Weite,
> Zur Liebsten musste, musste, weil sie zog,
> Gestirn und Nordschein über mir im Streite,
> Ich gehend, kommend Seligkeiten sog;
>   Um Mitternacht.
>
> Bis dann zuletzt des vollen Mondes Helle
> So klar und deutlich mir ins Finstere drang,
> Auch der Gedanke, willig, sinnig, schnelle
> Sich ums Vergangne wie ums Künftige schlang;
>   Um Mitternacht.

This poem, Goethe tells us, he always prized from the time when it came to him "in the middle of the night without premeditation"; and when we have entered into it and enjoyed, on the one hand, its fascinating negligence—the words and phrases being all released and relaxed, floating free from syntactical bondage among happy memories of the night-sky—and, on the other hand, the perfection of spiritual form which it traces in easy spiral flight from lesser illumination to greater till in the closing verse it embraces past, present, and future in a flood of light, we hardly need his word for it. There is something in these lines which he could not have forced, and which only the most affectionate of impulses could have produced. And it is all there in the poem, his sudden coming to it not less than his after-love for it.

What impresses us most in the poem is the immediacy,

the purity, with which Goethe has recorded his mood.
There is nothing in the grammatical looseness of the
sentences to suggest the self-conscious liberties of poets
who react against conventionality and disarrange their
poetic robes on purpose; the effect is far too subdued,
too unobtrusive, too convincing for that. What it
suggests is that Goethe has intercepted himself a little
sooner than usual and has managed to transcribe his
emotion before it has quite crystallized into logical
shape. The rare felicity of the poem is largely due to
its being thus conditioned and to its being perfectly
lucid at the same time. A minute earlier, we feel, and
it would have been confused; a minute later and it
would have lost its ingenuousness. We come so near
to the creative act that we almost feel that we are
made to share it.

Perhaps the most impressive instance of this kind of
writing is the poem, "Harzreise im Winter," of forty
years before—a poetic record, in eighty-eight short
rhymeless lines, of a journey Goethe took to the Brocken
in December 1777, opening with the strange invocation
"Let my song float like the vulture, which lies with
restful pinions on heavy clouds at morning, searching
for prey":

> Dem Geier gleich,
> Der auf schweren Morgenwolken
> Mit sanftem Fittich ruhend
> Nach Beute schaut,
> Schwebe mein Lied!

It so happens that we are unusually well informed of
the details of Goethe's life at this moment. One of the
various reasons for his journey to the Harz mountains
in this winter season was his desire to visit a misan-
thropic correspondent in Wernigerode, a certain Plessing
who had unbosomed himself by letter to Goethe and
had implored his advice and help—clearly a mental
case of the sort that was likely to interest the author of

Werther. Goethe's response was peculiar. He visited Plessing in person and gave him good counsel, but he did it incognito, as a chance caller, whom Plessing never suspected till afterwards. Something of the hot and the cold, the charitable and the diagnostic, in this curious adventure seems to have strayed into the opening image of the poem with its associations at once so relentless and so serene. And it is partly of Plessing that he is thinking when he goes on to contrast the happy lot of mortals with the unhappy; he is thinking of his own fortunate state as the lover of Charlotte, the confidential adviser of Karl August, and the friend of the Muses, and that of his morbid contemporary, eating his heart out with introspection in an obscure corner of the earth. An obvious thought. But what beauty and tenderness in the lines! "Who is it that goes aside? His path is lost in the bushes, the boughs close behind him, the grass stands up again, the waste swallows him. . . . O, loving Father, if there is a note on thy psaltery that his ears can hear, refresh his heart. Open his clouded gaze to the thousand wellsprings beside him in the desert":

> Aber abseits, wer ist's?
> Ins Gebüsch verliert sich sein Pfad,
> Hinter ihm schlagen
> Die Sträuche zusammen,
> Das Gras steht wieder auf,
> Die Öde verschlingt ihn.
>
> .   .   .   .
>
> Ist auf deinem Psalter,
> Vater der Liebe, ein Ton
> Seinem Ohre vernehmlich,
> So erquicke sein Herz!
> Öffne den umwölkten Blick
> Über die tausend Quellen
> Neben dem Durstenden
> In der Wüste!

The poem concludes with thoughts of himself, the

elect poet into whose songs all nature pours itself, and it ends with the image of his further destination, the Brocken, the mountain towering above its brethren and spilling its riches into the plains. Here, as in the vulture image at the beginning, the symbolical values are strongly felt. But they pervade the whole of this strange poem. These are the closing sentences: "With your dim torch you light him over the fords at night, through bottomless ways, in barren fields; with the myriad-coloured morning you laugh into his heart; with the biting storm you lift him aloft. The winter torrents leap from the rocks into his psalms, and the snow-hung summit of the fearsome mountain, crowned with ranks of spirits by the dreaming nations, is the altar on which he lays his thanks. You stand, inscrutable at heart, secret yet revealed, above an astonished world, and you look down from the clouds on its proud kingdoms which you water through the veins of your brothers about you":

> Mit der dämmernden Fackel
> Leuchtest du ihm
> Durch die Furten bei Nacht,
> Über grundlose Wege
> Auf öden Gefilden;
> Mit dem tausendfarbigen Morgen
> Lachst du ins Herz ihm;
> Mit dem beizenden Sturm
> Trägst du ihn hoch empor;
> Winterströme stürzen vom Felsen
> In seine Psalmen,
> Und Altar des lieblichsten Danks
> Wird ihm des gefürchteten Gipfels
> Schneebehangner Scheitel,
> Den mit Geisterreihen
> Kränzten ahnende Völker.

> Du stehst mit unerforschtem Busen
> Geheimnisvoll offenbar
> Über der erstaunten Welt
> Und schaust aus Wolken

Auf ihre Reiche und Herrlichkeit,
Die du aus den Adern deiner Brüder
Neben dir wässerst.

We can say of this poem what we can say of few—that the sense of its greatness reaches us before we have understood it; and while on a first reading it is obscure, the obscurity is wholly narrative and external and scarcely interferes with the lyrical values, which speak to our minds immediately and grow with every re-perusal. The elaborate interpretation which Goethe and others have supplied has intense biographical interest, and it enables us to follow in detail what happened and what went on in him. The setting out from Weimar northwards; the enigmatic journey to Wernigerode to visit Plessing; the ascent of the Brocken; the letters home to Charlotte; the geological lure of the hills—all this and more allows us to live these strangely exalted days in Goethe's life with great fullness and intimacy, yet it adds next to nothing to the poem, which towers serenely above its commentary and pours out its wealth of meaning regardless of it.

Here again, as in the briefer nocturne, it is the purity of communication which impresses us; these loosely connected paragraphs are what Goethe's creative mind exhaled during certain days of intense spiritual life; they are the distillation of himself transmitted directly to the written page, and not contaminated by the attendant detail which he took for granted, and which we may take for granted too, remembering that the pure gold of the poet's emotion has been given, and that the dross of explanation would only encumber it.

What we have traced in these two poems we can trace in others, and if we cannot always run it down with words we can feel that it is there or that something of it is there, pervading all the poems and making them distinctively Goethe's. If we live with these poems we find that they affect us as no others do. It is not so much that they are peculiar as that they put us into a peculiar relation to their author. Other poets to whom we come as readers betray their awareness of us, they seem to have anticipated our coming and to show it in their work. Either they put a play before us or they tell us a story, and if they are dramatic or epic poets they have to do one or the other. If they are lyrical poets, not under the same necessity of addressing any one, they are sure to exhort us or to shrink from us, or to pretend to ignore us, or in some way, by some subtle shade of accent or bearing, to make us feel that they are different because they have us in mind. Consequently we never see them exactly as they are, we only see them as they are for us. Either their art, as with the epic and dramatic poet, requires them to take cognizance of us as their necessary audience, or their conception of their art makes them choose to do so, or their personalities prevent them from doing otherwise and force them, even without their knowing it, to envisage an audience, a hearer, a somebody, so that never, or only at rare and fortunate moments, do they commune entirely with themselves or with their poem. However tightly they close the door, their creative sanctuary is never quite private; there is always someone sitting there, the *tertium quid*, waiting to hear the poem when the poet has finished with it. It is only Goethe who seems to be unaffected by us and, whenever the circumstances of his art allow, to retain that unself-consciousness which we all experience when we are sufficiently alone to forget that we are alone; and in this spirit he writes, not once or twice, or in flashes, or in restricted vein, but habitually, in age as in youth, and in all moods from the impetuous to the reflective, from the intimately self-communing to the authoritatively philosophical. The inimitable line from *Torquato Tasso*, "You feel the intention and are put off by it":

So fühlt man Absicht, und man ist verstimmt,

comes from him with a curious aptness; he is the one
poet whom the cap never fits.

It is the least obtrusive of miracles; we enter the room
where Goethe is sitting, and nothing is changed, he goes
on as before. If this was far from true of him in his
social bearing, it is unassailably true in the inner world
of his poetry, where he betrays a gift of unself-consciousness which we should not have thought possible if he had
not demonstrated it. It belongs in the first place to
the world of his shorter poems, where it is easiest to
sustain, and where we shall search in vain for the calcu-
ated—or, what is just as self-conscious—the inten-
tionally uncalculated effects of other poets. But it is
not there only. Something of this central quality
accompanies him everywhere in his poetic life and
leavens what he writes, enabling him to compose moral
epigrams which have all the comfortableness of anony-
mous proverbs, not directed at any one, but simply
existing for what they may be worth, and to carry out
his gigantic project of *Faust* without being guilty of a
syllable of rhetoric—an amazing achievement when we
consider the temptations latent in the theme and the
response another poet, say Byron, would have made
to them. We have only to compare Goethe's work with
Schiller's at the time of their great partnership to feel
that even here, where he is drawn farthest from his
poetic habits by this close association with a poetic
mind diametrically opposed to his, he remains true to
his instincts and seldom deserts them for long. Look
where we may we shall find that we, the readers, never
seriously interfere with him, the poet, but that he
manages to say what he has to say for its own sake and
for his, not merely losing conscious thought of us—
others can do that—but entirely eliminating us at the
moment of saying it.

There were times when he realized something of this
and was even embarrassed by it. He could not help

writing poetry; again and again it came from him with irresistible force; yet when he wrote he had no choice but to be off his guard. He could not clothe himself in the self-consciousness, the rhetoric, of other poets; whatever he wrote had to come in a state of forgetfulness of all else. He might dissemble at other times, but not when he wrote poetry. That is why he says half regretfully in one of the *Divan* poems that "it is useless for a poet to be reticent," that "poetry is itself a betrayal":

> Dichter ist umsonst verschwiegen,
> Dichten selbst ist schon Verrat,

and in *Faust* he lets the spokesman for poetry say it again, but this time with pride, "I do not act in secret, I only need to breathe and I am betrayed":

> Nicht insgeheim vollführ' ich meine Taten,
> Ich atme nur, und schon bin ich verraten.

It is by virtue of this quality in his work, disconcerting though it was when he reflected on it, that he was able to set himself down with such wonderful veracity. He was too good a poet to tie himself pedantically to facts and details. We shall find silences in his poetic account of himself, we shall find fiction in it, we shall find what are called inaccuracies. But in essential truth it is such that we may doubt whether all the researches of a century have either added to it or taken away from it.

CHAPTER VIII

THE DEFEAT OF CONVENTION

NOTHING that Goethe has said about his poetry lends itself more readily to misinterpretation than the famous pronouncement in his autobiography that his works were "fragments of a great confession" (Bruchstücke einer grossen Konfession). Confession, taken in its usual sense, is the last word we should think of applying to him; neither absolutely nor historically can we accept it at its face value. If he had been an author of the type established in modern literature by Rousseau, if he had written with the intention of confessing, if his poetry had been prompted by the need of communicating his mind to another mind and thereby vindicating itself, his work would bear the marks of it; it would address us, it would solicit our regard, it would ask to be read. But no. What we find is the reverse of this—a poetry so rich in the opposite virtue, so unprecedented in its pervasive quality of neither seeking its reader nor avoiding him nor in any way involving him, that we lack words to describe it.

Only in a secondary sense can the word "confession" be allowed to stand. Being intimately lyrical and personal—a betrayal of himself, as Goethe put it—his poetry is the equivalent of a confession, it tells us what he would have told us if he had been minded to confess. But this is all. The so-called confession is the inevitable consequence of his creative act and has nothing to do with the act itself, which, if we are to judge by the distinctive temper of the poetry which it produces, remains strangely self-contained, self-communing. The more we read this poetry, coming to it now from this author and now from that and slowly learning to see it from many angles, the more does it impress us with its inner completeness, its rounded life, its unique self-fulfilment.

If we restore the phrase "fragments of a great confession" to its context—it is usually quoted out of context—there is no difficulty. "And so," he writes, "there began that tendency, which I could never deviate from all my life, to turn what delighted or tortured or otherwise occupied me into an image or a poem and be done with it, both in order to correct my notions of outer things, and to compose myself inwardly. No one needed this gift more than I, because my nature flung me continually from one extreme to the other. Thus, all my works are fragments of a great confession. . . ."

It is clear from this passage—and the larger context makes it clearer still—that Goethe did not intend to stamp his poetry as confessional, and that he gives us no real authority for doing so. What he says, if we read him closely, is that he wrote it as a reckoning with himself, and that its confessional aspect follows from this. It is the reckoning with himself that is characteristic, not the confession. For while the impulse to write for oneself, to free oneself by writing, far from being unknown to others, is perhaps the primary poetic impulse, and there is no poet great or small who has not felt it and acted on it; in Goethe this impulse operates with a cogency and a persistence which puts him in a class apart. Instead of turning into an accomplishment, a vocation, a faculty separate and circumscribed, as poetry usually does, Goethe's poetry retains from first to last its crucial importance—functional more than cathartic—for his mental and bodily health. It is as deeply rooted in him as the instinct for food and the instinct for sleep; it is equally necessary to him; and it operates with the same infallibility. Given the required

crisis in his life, the poetry will come of itself. It is
regulative, preservative. When he needs to sleep he
sleeps, and when he needs to write poetry he writes
poetry. No sooner does the stress of joy or sorrow, the
turmoil of doubt, the tension of deep insight become
acute than the poetic instinct awakens in him and
helps to correct the disturbance.

The most famous example is that of *Werther* which,
by giving expression to the suicide mood incidental to
his early emotionalism, liberated him and restored him
to a more normal state of mind. But what it is less
easy to believe, though he says it himself, is that this
controlling function is at the bottom of all his poetry
and is as vital to him at the end of his life as it was at
the beginning. There is conclusive evidence of this in
the last of his love-poems. The "Trilogie der Leidenschaft," written in his seventy-fourth and seventy-fifth
years at the time of his fantastically hopeless passion
for Ulrike von Levetzow, is, if anything, more necessary
to him, more a matter of life and death, than the *Werther*
which he wrote at twenty-four. Here, in his waning
life, we can say more confidently than in his youth that
if he had lacked the power "to say what he suffered"
he would have gone to pieces.

There is this interesting difference between *Werther*
and the "Trilogie der Leidenschaft"—the earliest and
the latest of the greater emotional crises recorded in
Goethe's poetry—that the recording of the latter crisis
frankly recognizes and expresses its vital function and
shapes itself accordingly, while in *Werther* the function
is implicit and not immediately discoverable. It is
only by reading the commentaries to *Werther* that we
can arrive at anything more than conjecture as to its
private relation to Goethe, and it is only because we
have his express word for it that we know for certain
that he healed the sickness of his spirit by writing
it down.

This is true of the poetic works as a whole. They do not tell us in so many words why they came into existence. It is only in the "Trilogie der Leidenschaft" that the poetry lets out its secret at a crucial moment, though there was a hint of it at the close of *Torquato Tasso*. Here at last, in obedience to that growing explicitness of his poetic life manifested in the final stages in the writing of *Faust*, Goethe states in his own verses and in the midst of his anguish—the words occur at the end of the first of the three poems—that he sings to save himself and that, like his own Tasso, he must look to his power of self-expression to free him from his present torment. "How touching it is when the poet sings to escape the death that comes at parting! A prey to these torments, and not free from blame, may he be given the power to say what he endures":

> Wie klingt es rührend, wenn der Dichter singt,
> Den Tod zu meiden, den das Scheiden bringt!
> Verstrickt in solche Qualen, halbverschuldet,
> Geb' ihm ein Gott, zu sagen, was er duldet.

And it is part of the same explicitness when he arranges the three poems so as to express both the crisis and the recovery from it, reversing the order which they take in date of composition and giving them as a connected whole the spiritual movement and consummation which his poetry had enabled him to achieve in his person a hundred times, but which he had never before so lucidly conveyed in the poetry itself. First we read the announcement of the passion, couched in the form of an address to the ghost of Werther, who comes from the grave to commune with his progenitor, the dead facing the living across the deep gulf of years; next the Elegy, the Marienbad Elegy, rehearsing the last meeting of the lovers—the anticipation, the fulfilment, the parting, the misery—and then deliberately seeking the means of recovery—in the splendour of the outer world, "Is not the world left? Are not the rocks still crowned with sacred shadows? Is there not the harvest?"

> Ist denn die Welt nicht übrig? Felsenwände,
> Sind sie nicht mehr gekrönt von heiligen Schatten?
> Die Ernte, reift sie nicht?

in illusory dreams of her whom he has lost, in the deeper truth of his abiding recollection of her as she was, in the ultimate values which he can extract from this great memory. Yet all in vain, the experience crushes him as it crushed Werther, and the Elegy ends on a note of despair, leaving it to the concluding poem to resolve the despair, and with healing music to lead the sufferer back to life and the acceptance of life.

What Goethe's poetry does for him here at the nadir of tribulation we must imagine it doing also at the zenith of happiness. He tells us that "everything on earth can be endured, except a succession of happy days":

> Alles in der Welt lässt sich ertragen,
> Nur nicht eine Reihe von schönen Tagen,

and we can see from this and from other indications that the inner necessity would be as great at this extreme as at the extreme of suffering. Among the happiest days which Goethe has recorded are those which produced the *West-östlicher Divan*, and here, more than in any other extensive body of his verse, we can feel its tonic quality as we read it. There is something inimitable about it at this stage. Marianne von Willemer—the inspirer of the *Divan*—was more nearly his spiritual mate, more nearly a woman of genius, than any other woman he had known intimately, and she was pledged to one who was both her benefactor and his friend. It was the old Werther triangle again, and just as precarious. Yet this time all passes off serenely and even joyfully with no aftertaste of bitterness, no frustration. And while this comfortable issue must be ascribed in part to niceties of temperament and affinity which we are not

L

in a position to investigate, something must also be due to the restorative virtue of the poetic life, which in this case operated with surprising ease and felicity. It so happened that Marianne had poetic gifts as well as he, and this quickly opened the poetic vein in him and made it a part of their intercourse, so that day by day the wings of poetry lifted them and made the hard ground light beneath their feet. There are moments of tragedy here, but they are quickly expressed and mastered, while the prevailing mood is one of exhilaration, rising now and then to sublimer flights, but for the most part disporting itself adroitly in unambitious situations. There is a perennial fascination in these verses, transcending somehow their intrinsic merits; nowhere else shall we find the game of poetry lending itself to such delicate mastery of life. Only because he can be Hatem and she Suleika can they venture so nimbly where others would fear to tread, and it is this secret knowledge, this expert connivance in wisdom, which gives the *Divan* verses their special flavour, making them sometimes playful, sometimes cryptic, but always bracing and cordial like the wines they celebrate.

We can see now why Goethe's poems should affect us so differently from the general run of poems, good and bad. Being so vital an exercise of his nature they habitually spend themselves in their relation to him, and are able to ignore, if not to dispense with, the communicative elements which so readily associate themselves with the poetic art. If Goethe's verses seem to be strangely independent of any recipient, and to make us feel again and again that he would have written them just the same if he had been suddenly alone in the world, it is because Goethe, the producer of them, is his own recipient. Writing because he must— in obedience to an organic law stronger and more persistent in him than in any other human being we know— he establishes a kind of creative life which returns upon itself and comes to rest or to fulfilment at or near the point at which it started.   This is a poetry which turns on its own axis, it is like the forest which fertilizes itself with its own leaves, it is the mysterious and emblematic snake which circles itself tail to mouth, knowing good and evil.

It is natural that a poet so constituted should take his poetry for granted.   Goethe does this.   He is at heart the most nonchalant of authors, writing his verses as a matter of course when he is impelled to write them, and remaining unperplexed when the impulse deserts him. He is as little concerned in his inner mind with the worth and the prestige of his poetry after he has made it as he is reluctant to woo it, force it, organize it, before he has made it.   The poet's pride, the poet's ambition, scarcely touches him in all his long lifetime.   We shall look in vain in his writings for the note of Horace's "aere perennius," or of Shakespeare's

> Not marble nor the gilded monuments
> Of princes shall outlive this powerful rhyme,

or Ronsard's "Quand tu seras bien vieille . . ." or Hölderlin's "Grant me a summer and an autumn, you mighty ones, for my ripe song":

> Nur einen Sommer gönnt, ihr Gewaltigen,
> Und einen Herbst zu reifem Gesange mir.

It would be as unnatural in Goethe to sound this note as to pray that his life might be prolonged in order that he might sleep.   When he imagines himself entering the Mohammedan paradise and the houri at the gate demands his credentials, he submits his common humanity and asks for no favours as a poet.   "Stop this fussing and let me in, for I was a man, and that means a fighter":

> Nicht so vieles Federlesen!
> Lass mich immer nur herein:
> Denn ich bin ein Mensch gewesen,
> Und das heisst ein Kämpfer sein.

And if we go back forty years to the days when he was burgeoning with promise and might be expected to display his consciousness of it, we shall find that this indifferent and unprofessional attitude must have been his from the beginning. In the only poem of these years in which he expresses the desire to create—he never expresses it again—he does so merely in the interests of a fuller life and with little thought of artistic achievement. His mind passes quickly from thoughts of art to thoughts of nature, insight, experience, and he ends, "O Nature, how I long for you, long to feel you truly! For me you will be a merry fountain, playing from a thousand jets. You will make all your powers bright in my mind and extend my narrow existence into an eternity ":

> Wie sehn' ich mich, Natur, nach dir,
> Dich treu und lieb zu fühlen!
> Ein lust'ger Springbrunn wirst du mir
> Aus tausend Röhren spielen.
>
> Wirst alle deine Kräfte hier
> In meinem Sinn erheitern
> Und dieses enge Dasein mir
> Zur Ewigkeit erweitern.

And so it is everywhere. Tasso's concern is with the problem of living, and his pride as a poet only awakens under the deliberate taunts of Antonio or under pangs of suffering which compel him to remember that he has the poet's resources to fall back on.

This suggests a certain subordination of poetry to other interests. Goethe, it is sometimes argued, put life first and poetry second and is therefore less completely a poet than those who reversed the order and wrote poetry at all costs. But this does not follow. It is true that he subordinated his poetry, but he did not subordinate it to anything extraneous—as, it might be claimed, all poets do who in any way professionalize themselves and write to earn money, or to instil patriotism, or to teach morals, or to propound an idea. By referring it to its proper fount and origin he simply emphasized a subordination which already existed in the nature of poetry, and in this sense it could be held that he made his poetry more fundamental and was therefore the truer poet. For that matter, it is as impossible to imagine Goethe renouncing the writing of poetry, or losing the power to write it, as to imagine him contemplating the loss of it or fearing lest it should fail him in any ambition. There were periods when he wrote little, and there were periods when he wrote nothing, yet the faculty was latent in him all the time and was not less powerful at the end of his life, though the crises were fewer, than it had been at the beginning. The picture of Goethe writing a Farewell to Poesy or breaking his staff and drowning his book for good and all is one which we cannot visualize. It was not in his power to say at any moment that he would write—except perfunctorily, as he sometimes did—and it was still less in his power to say that he would not write, since the compelling need might arise at any moment. The poetic art is wholly natural to him, more natural to him probably than to any other poet, and he treats it accordingly.

Any study of Goethe's management of poetic convention must begin at this point. Having by sheer naturalness avoided, outwitted, defeated the most elementary form of conventionality in poetry—that conscious or half-conscious recognition of a potential hearer which establishes at the outset a change of mood in the poet corresponding to the very similar change in real life—Goethe proceeds to do the same with the more elaborate forms of it. The unself-consciousness which enabled him spontaneously to execute "Um Mitternacht" or "Harzreise im Winter"—or, if further examples are needed, "Versunken" from the *Divan*, or "Tagebuch (1810)," the latter an almost unbelievably natural treatment of an erotic theme—underlies all his workmanship, and can be discovered in it, no matter what phase or aspect of it we explore.

Consider his use of metre. Only the most perfunctory examination is needed to establish Goethe among the richest and happiest of metrists. Give him time and he will entertain you with the freest of free verse, the severest of unfree; the extremes of the colloquial and the formal; German doggerel, Latin elegiac, Italian sonnet, or Persian ghazal. There is no end to it. *Faust* itself is a treasure-house of metrical adventure; on this score alone Goethe is a supreme master of verse-forms. Yet it is only by an effort that we bring ourselves to say it, and in reading the poetry we become conscious of it at one moment only to forget it the next. Far from drawing our attention to this aspect of itself—as Milton's or Victor Hugo's poetry does—this poetry consistently distracts us from it. Just as there are people whose unusual bearing and vitality prevents us from studying their features in the act of talking to them, so these verses by their very character prevent us from merely looking at them and make us unconscious of their appearance as we read them.

There can only be one explanation. The creative reader duplicates the act of the creative poet and finds in the effect the poems have on him the key to the state of mind which made them. Goethe, we must infer, came naturally by this metrical flexibility and was not studious of it. The poetry seems to tell us this, and we have ample proof besides. This master of verse-forms, we find, is a tiro in prosody; as soon as he becomes conscious of the technique of his verses he is a child and must manage to forget the technique if he is to recover his mastery of it. His words to Herder in a letter accompanying the manuscript of *Iphigenie auf Tauris*, now ready for publication, are such as no academic prosodist and few poets of any sort could have written. He tells Herder that there are lines which still dissatisfy him, and he gives him a free hand to make such changes in them as he thinks desirable. This was a work upon which Goethe had brought himself metrically to a standstill. The problem of converting it from its iambic prose into regular blank verse was one that he had waited most of ten years to solve, so incapable was he of playing the technician and coolly polishing his lines. And when in the end he studies the theory of prosody and learns the rules of the game, he brings himself to a deadlock and is willing at the last moment to surrender his text—or parts of it—to the tender mercies of another.

The meaning of this is clear. The rules had to be in his bones if they were to be of use to him, the book-knowledge paralysed him. We shall find in *Iphigenie auf Tauris* effects of metre, rhythm, word-music fit to stand with the best in poetry, yet they are essentially unstudied, they came of themselves; he forgot the rules in order to write them. Orestes' line which says that the fresh faces about him soon "betray the marks of a creeping death,"

Den Schmerzenszug langsamen Tods verraten,

with its pained sibilants, its transposed and retarding middle foot, and its ominous closing vowels, has all the merits the prosodist could give it, yet we cannot take it as an example of Goethe's virtuosity, because he wrote it as iambic prose and lifted it bodily into his blank verse without altering a syllable.

If we ask why he chooses blank verse at this point the answer is all of a piece with the rest; it is not an arbitrary choice, such as Lessing made when he adopted blank verse as the suitable dramatic metre for Germans, or such as Schiller made when he decided that Lessing was right and followed suit; it is an instinctive choice prompted by deeper motives. For while it is true that Goethe first toyed with blank verse as an alternative to alexandrines, and we possess a few lines about an early tragedy, *Belsazer*, in evidence of it, he was young and precocious then, and had not found himself. When he came seriously to this metre it was with the spirit of Charlotte von Stein upon him. To express that spirit it was as natural for him to hit upon blank verse as to hit upon the story of Tasso, not because it was a useful metre for elevated drama, but because in a European perspective it was a Renaissance metre, and appropriate to the mood of Renaissance idealism with which she had filled him. When this mood has spent itself Goethe drops the metre and rarely writes it again; without the emotional justification he cannot use it.

This analysis holds good for all Goethe's metres, even the folk-metres which he came upon so early. If he adopts the forms of folk-poetry it is not because they are an attractive convention which promises to be fashionable, but because he is filled full of folk-poetry. Herder talks to him about it by the hour, he roams the villages around Strassburg and copies it down from the lips of the peasantry, and with all this vivid actuality behind him he writes or refashions the "Heidenröslein," he writes the "König in Thule" and a few other pieces —a handful in all—returning to folk-poetry at rare moments in later life to write a "Blümlein Wunderschön," and show that the spirit of it is in him all the time, even when he seems farthest from it, but never writing it as a habit, never in all his long life repeating himself in it. In this he stands in vivid contrast with the younger German poets of his day, and especially with Heine, who so brilliantly adapted the folk-song to the purposes of his sophisticated lyricism, and then used it and used it till it wearied him, and he dropped it from utter satiety.

This natural use of metre is not uncommon in poets

who, like Shakespeare, stick chiefly to one metre and use it as a matter of routine. Goethe—and this is what makes his case unique—uses all imaginable metres, and is incapable of routine; look where we may we shall fail to find either mere routine or mere experiment in his changes of form. If he touches the sonnet, he has been drawn to it by a tentative love-affair and intimacy with a sonnet-loving circle; it is more than literary adventuring with him, his heart is in it. The elegiacs of his middle years, permanently rooted though they seem, fall away from him in due course; and lighter, looser metres replace them, more attuned to the growing exhilaration of his late sixties. He evolves a new metre to suit a new theme, and having used it once with consummate appropriateness he has done with it for good; his two most noble ballads, "Die Braut von Korinth" and "Der Gott und die Bajadere," both exemplify this. The consequence is that we never accept what may seem to be an arbitrary choice of metre, as we would unhesitatingly in another, without asking ourselves what deeper motives may account for it. Twice Goethe uses *terza rima*—once to convey the monologue on the Alpine rainbow in *Faust*, and again to convey his aged thoughts at the sight of Schiller's skull. In the first case he may have remembered the dazzling close of the "Paradiso," he may have felt the need and the fitness of an Italian metre to express the southward movement of his poem; in the second case he may have preferred an exacting and unpractised metre to give him artificial steadiness in face of the visible signs of corruption which confronted his poetic mind, and which—as we know from other occasions—he involuntarily shrank from with an almost animal fear. None of these explanations may suffice, yet we are compelled to inquire in this spirit, because we can be nearly certain that Goethe was incapable of making a purely conventional choice of metre, and of fitting his thoughts to it. But for this the remarks of Simmel on the discrepancy between the content of the Marienbad Elegy and its metre would have little meaning. At first sight the metre—a plain six-line stanza, with alternate rhymes and then a couplet—is acceptable enough, and it is only when we realize that it lacks the Goethean inevitability that we are in a position to understand Simmel's explanation. This metre, he says, is as the comparative impotence of old age coping with the spring-floods of love, the youth and the senility of this tragic episode being reflected in the clash of form and mood. Thus the very inadequacy of the metre gives it its deeper expressiveness and truth.

There is only one signal and sustained instance of prosodic self-consciousness in Goethe, and it is a most welcome one, because it is an exception which not only proves the rule, but requires it. In the Helena act of *Faust* the metres are so profound in significance that it is they rather than the *dramatis personæ* which express and carry on the action. The Greek trimeter, in which Helena addresses us—it is anticipated by Erichtho's speech at the beginning of the Classical Walpurgisnacht and remembered in Faust's words at the beginning of Act IV—is as indispensable as Helena herself. Without this metre of hers we should not experience the actuality which Goethe intends, we should not recognize her for the very thing of beauty that Hellas knew. It is only through the trimeter and the choric rhythms that alternate with it that Goethe is able to bring back the Athenian drama with any sense of its poetic reality. Put this passage into prose, and its meaning evaporates. And in the later passage where Faust teaches Helena to speak in rhyme the meaning passes wholly into the metrical form, and a prose rendering would destroy it outright. Here, we might say, is metre used more consciously and with a completer sophistication than ever before by any poet. But we can also say with

equal truth that it is metre elevated into a symbol of
the changing spirit of man and purged as never before
of all mere externality. It is only because Goethe's
apprehension of metre is so much more than conventional
that he is able thus to dramatize it, and to invest trimeter
and couplet and stanza with a speaking force greater at
moments than that of the characters who use them.

It is the same everywhere, in plot structure as in
metrical structure. Goethe rarely complies with the
conventional standards of dramatic and narrative
literature, and he never complies in longer works without
forfeiting something of his power. The mastery which
he achieves with superb ease in short poems, lyrical and
narrative, he cannot attempt with impunity on a larger
scale. He shows in his early drama, *Clavigo*, that he
has all Schiller's knack of stage dialogue; the conversation between Carlos and Clavigo, in which the vacilla-
ting lover is masterfully swayed by the subtle rhetoric
and the stronger will of his unscrupulous friend, is as well
handled as any in *Kabale und Liebe*, and the whole play
is theatrically effective. Yet we cannot say that the
real Goethe is in it. It has neither the vernal freshness
of *Götz von Berlichingen*, nor the felicity of his early
lyrics, nor the mysterious power of *Werther* and the
Urfaust; and it has no qualities of its own to compare
with these for a moment. *Clavigo* impresses us rather
as a good and promising work by some other author that
has strayed by accident into Goethe's pages than as an
authentic and unmistakable piece of himself; it will be
best appreciated by those who wish Goethe had been
otherwise, and who deplore the possible frustration in
him of a talent for drama; but in the end it will be found
to contribute little or nothing to his true stature. Thus
the cleverest of Goethe's early writings is his least
worthy.

In the one other notable instance in which he makes a
drama conform satisfactorily to the accepted standards,

he also pays a price. When Iphigenie tells the truth to Thoas and precipitates the final crisis of the play, we have to admit that the inevitability of great drama is lacking, that this crisis is not necessitated as the strangling of Desdemona is necessitated, because Iphigenie's relations with Thoas are such that she might have told him quietly and obtained her wish. Remembering Thoas's given word that she was free to return to Greece when the opportunity came, we might say that this less dramatic solution would have been more convincing. But in order to drive home a moral idea, and to round off his play—each of these intentions is foreign to him at other times—Goethe forces upon the situation a tension and uncertainty which it hardly warrants and thereby falls short of the highest that is in him.

His narrative art is like his dramatic; it succeeds in proportion as it is not careful to conform. *Hermann und Dorothea*, by far his outstanding achievement in the art of sustained story-telling, does not hold us to-day as the amorphous *Werther* holds us or the philosophically overloaded *Wahlverwandtschaften*. The failure of this beautifully conducted idyll of German life to endear itself as it should, even to those who are native to it, is not so much the fault of its somewhat alien hexameters as of its comparative lack of depth. Its formal mastery —slightly marred by the intrusion of the theme of the French Revolution, which, instead of underlying the poem, seems to be superimposed upon it here and there, but nevertheless a real and incontestable mastery— cannot blind us to the fact that the poem sees no deeper into life than it is given to lesser poets to see, and that here, as before, Goethe loses more than he gains when he sets out to compose as others do, be it never so skilfully. *Werther*, we may admit, cannot compare with *Hermann und Dorothea* in narrative technique; its concluding pages are its least convincing pages, they remind us that the poet had finished before the story-teller and that the poet was the stronger of the two. Yet if we are to choose whom we shall sit with at the well it must be the melancholy Werther, not the estimable Hermann and Dorothea, for he sees more than they, and his words are undying.

Everything goes to show that Goethe excels when he defeats the conventions, whether by breaking with them as he does in the best of his longer works, or by fulfilling them unawares as he almost invariably does in short poems. When he is complying with the conventions expressly he is seldom or never at his best. The virtue of his poetry is in the pure organic impulse which sets it going, and if he has a technique it is the technique of guarding this impulse, of carrying it up into the working-out of the poems, and, as far as possible, of letting it write them. This does not mean that in the final result he dispenses with convention; that is beyond the power of any poet, and Goethe, as his work shows, would be the last to desire it. It means that a convention has to be second nature with him before he can use it to advantage; he must assimilate and digest it, and wait for it to come as part of the initial impulse, flowing with it and strengthening its flow, rather than as some improvized dam or filter which erects itself against the impulse and deprives it of its momentum.

Incredible as it may sound when we consider Goethe's range and variety, this is the technique, the inner technique, of all his work, no matter how cultured, deliberate, and sophisticated it becomes. The technique may be less perfect in one case than another; the longer the poem the less capable it is of dispensing with inorganic elements. Yet the truth remains that Goethe practised this technique from first to last, and that it is the essential technique of every piece of his verse, long or short, that we value for its own sake.

This technique, this way of dealing with himself, was forced upon him by his literary environment. There was no easy tradition for him to drop into as there was for Shakespeare, no obvious and excellent themes for him to treat, no ready mould to pour them into. The only alternative to the kind of poetry he elected was a highly artificial, arbitrary poetry, such as Schiller produced when by sheer will and intellect he established a tradition of verse-drama in Germany which owed nothing to the world about it and was entirely based on moral and literary judgments. This was possible for Schiller, and it was commendable in him; but for Goethe it was not to be thought of. His nature precluded it and left him no choice but to grow everything within himself, to create in himself the environment which failed him in the literary world. He sometimes deplored this condition—as well he might when we consider the immense spiritual endeavour which it entailed—and regretted that he was not born into a more poetic age, in which the stage was set and the audience ready. Yet we can only rejoice that it was not so, and that Goethe was compelled by the world about him to be the poet he was.

If he had only known it he was fortunate in his disadvantages. A nature poet, if ever there was one, he had no exhausting problem of poetic diction to wrestle with, as Wordsworth had. The conventional language and the literary fashion which he had followed in his early Leipzig poetry was the shallowest imaginable; it trafficked in the emptiest of conceits, the most tenuous of pastoral superficialities. It was the negation of the Goethean ideal, as we now see it. Goethe acquired it all in a flash and even turned out a little masterpiece or two of precocious virtuosity. His "Brautnacht" beats the withered old poetasters at their own game. Yet when the moment came to break with it, it might never have existed. He turned his back on it and wrote as if he had never known it; he never echoes it involuntarily, he never reacts against it, he is

completely free from it. And, what is more, he finds
the poetic resources of the language virtually untapped.
Born, as he was, into the later eighteenth century, he
found waiting for his magic touch a poetic vocabulary
with all the bloom and dew of an unspoilt world upon it.
When he writes of love blessing "the fresh fields and
the teeming world, asmoke with flowers,"

> Du segnest herrlich
> Das frische Feld,
> Im Blütendampfe
> Die volle Welt,

he enters into a verbal inheritance as little worn by
usage as Walther von der Vogelweide's six hundred
years before him. It is as fresh as Chaucer's; there
seems to be no conventional verbiage to reckon with.
Klopstock and others who were true poets before him
seem rather to have loosened the soil about the poetic
resources of modern German than to have quite un-
earthed them, and it was left to Goethe to discover them
as if none had done it before him. The Klopstockian
reminiscences here and there in his early poetic speech
are as nothing beside its freshly germinating, sprouting
life; the words come breaking through the mould like
the spring grass and flowers. There was something in
the language when he picked it up which relieved him
of all dilemma; he could write with no thought of what
was poetic or not poetic, and with no fear of recalling
others unconsciously and finding what many modern
poets have found—that the return to nature was
blocked by the sophistication of the speech-medium
they were compelled to use, that the echoes of other
poets lay too thickly about the words they had heard
in their cradles for them ever to succeed in liberating
themselves from the dead hand of the past.

We see then that Goethe—though he was perhaps
the only poet who was capable of despising the language

he wrote in—was ideally situated for the task he was born to fulfil, because his almost miraculous defeating of convention would have been itself defeated if he had not had a clean palette and a clean canvas to work with. For this reason alone a French Goethe, or even an English Goethe, could never have been; their better opportunities would have robbed them of the great opportunity. It was only the peculiar retarding of German culture and the consequent paucity of literary tradition that made it possible for Goethe to exist in the modern world as the unprecedented poet we now know him to be. To an extent which we should have thought impossible his work is at once highly cultured and wholly natural; it contains all the conventions of the past; all the forms, metres, and literary devices of all the ages find their way into it sooner or later; but never a conventional way, for everything is re-experienced and re-made. The whole of his poetry from the simple to the elaborate, and from the raw experience in life to its highest formal refinement in art, is organic in one and the same sense, and the inorganic or less perfectly organic elements which we find in other poetry are negligible or non-existent.

Thus Goethe's poetic mind was marvellously true to its kindred points—true to the self which speaks and to the nature which prompts. He sanctioned nothing that was not his by more than intellectual right, and he sanctioned nothing that was not also natural. And by satisfying the one standard he satisfied the other. By seeing to it that all he expressed was a part of himself he put nature's stamp on it; and by seeing to it that all he expressed was natural he made it his own. The poetic instrument which he discovered and perfected was the ideal instrument for the recording of himself and, through himself, of nature. Of the three items —nature, his art, himself—the first had to be taken as it was; the second was as good as he could make it;

everything hung upon the third item, which was Goethe. And in the Herculean task of getting the last ounce out of himself he had the secret thought to sustain him that whatever he truly experienced he could set down in poetry with less loss in the telling than any man before or since.

CHAPTER IX

THE SCALE OF BEING

THE situation would have been wasted on a poet of narrow range. Once such a poet had gone the little round of himself he would have had to choose between holding his peace henceforth or in some way or other, either in the form of his writing or in the experience which he brought to it, repeating himself and thereby admitting the element of convention into his work which all poets, except Goethe, have been compelled to admit sooner or later, unless they admitted it at the start. It was essential to the fulfilment of Goethe's genius that he should be continually moving into new pastures, never settling down to any habit of poetry, but at every turn establishing some original confrontation of nature and self, as pure and as immediate "as on Creation's day," and that, failing this, he should remain scrupulously silent, as he often did. If Goethe had not grown in poetry to the end he would not have written to the end. We do not know the exact range of his poetic genius; all we know is that he spent sixty-odd years exploring it, or waiting for it to unfold, and that he was breaking new ground and discovering new resources in himself when his life stopped.

But what kind of ground and what kind of resources it is not so easy to state, though it is clear that the answer must be in terms of poetic quality rather than in terms of theme and plot. To satisfy ourselves of this we have only to remember that the Faust theme dragged on with him to the last, that he toyed with the Prometheus and Pandora story in old age as he had toyed with it in youth, and that he never at any time of life showed the business-like eagerness to dispatch one

subject and plunge into another, which enabled Schiller
to complete a whole cycle of dramas while he was merely
adding to one. Fertile in invention as Goethe was, he
made no attempt to compete with other poets in the
elaborating of incident; where he excelled was in the
variety of ways in which he succeeded in apprehending
the world, the psychological flexibility which enabled
him to adapt himself as a poet to all that he encountered
in his long and amazingly comprehensive experience of
men and things.

This is the key to his various poetic researches into
the work of others, whether in early life into folk-song
or Ossian—not great poetry, but a definite type of poetry
—or later into Propertius, Homer, Hafiz, or the Chinese
lyricism which he was beginning to acquire in his last
years. In all these cases, and in others that might be
instanced, we shall find that he does not approach his
predecessors in order to emulate them or copy them
superficially, but to experience them, to adjust his
sense-perceptions to theirs, to let their rhythm, their
idiosyncrasy, their consciousness, pass into him; and in
this way to know the mystery of existence as they knew
it. If in his penetration of Homer his deeper intention
had been to write epics in the Homeric manner, he
would have assuredly written them, for there was
nothing to stop him. But no. No sooner has he fully
equipped himself for the task than he loses interest in it.
A short idyll of German life in Homeric hexameters and
—more significant—a short excursion into the Homeric
world, and his ambition is satisfied or so nearly satisfied
that he writes no more in this vein. He has mastered
the Homeric sensibility, he has added the Homeric
apprehension of things to his many other apprehensions,
and having done this he moves on, slowly, imperceptibly,
to new experiences.

These researches of Goethe's are unlike those of any
other poet. It is not for him a question of apprentice-

ship, of feeling his way with one poet after another with a view to finding the kind of poetry best suited to his genius or most likely to content one who had no style of his own. No doubt he began somewhat blindly in this spirit; his early and imperfectly successful excursion into Shakespeare may be regarded in this light. But we cannot say this of the later cases, particularly those that came with Italy and after Italy, because it is clear by this time that he had found himself as surely as any poet we know, and that he was firmly established in a poetic universe of his own. Nor can we regard these incidents in his poetic life as divagations or experiments such as a poet of his learning and curiosity might be excused for making, because, as we have seen, the forces at work in Goethe's nature were invariably more than those of the craftsman or the dilettante and it was not given to him to make what we call literary choices at all. Wherever we find him seriously occupied with the work of another poet, we shall find that his nature is responding to the other's and growing to meet it, and that some profound modification or extension of his sensibility is the result.

And seeing that these occasions came—not frequently, but inevitably—both early and late in the course of his long life, we are compelled to recognize that the line of his genius did not run parallel to other poets, as we should expect, but across them, intersecting first one and then another, and breaking down all our known classifications, not merely of poetic forms and styles, but even of poetic personalities. Goethe's journey as a poet is not through any given field of experience that can be stated in terms of literary genre, or of fable, or even of temperament, it is through experience itself, through consciousness, through the variations of consciousness; and in making this unprecedented journey it was but natural that he should approach the mentality of other poets, and that he should occasionally attach himself to one of these and use him as a temporary anchorage. And in this spirit he dwells at one time with Tasso, at another with Propertius, at another with Hafiz, not always on the same terms nor with the same degree of self-surrender, but always with deep insight and intimacy and—unlike his antithesis, the eclectic poet—always at the one and only time in his career when this insight and this intimacy were possible for him.

For making this transit of the poetic life Goethe was magnificently equipped. Our final impression of him is that the scope of his nature was unbounded and that, given the requisite prolongation of years and energy, his personality would have been adequate to the experiencing of all forms of poetic sensibility whatsoever. In the time allotted to him he may be said to have covered no small part of the total ground, and to have touched some of the extreme points of differentiation, so that any further development would have been rather a filling-out of the gaps than an extending of the frontiers.

The range of poetic sensibility established in this one mind by the simple Strassburg love-songs and the esoteric choruses in *Pandora*, by the spontaneous beginning and the deliberate close of *Faust*, and by the diffuse prose-poetry of *Werther* and the firm distichs of the *Roman Elegies*, is without rival or precedent in the field of great poetry. All other great poets—Shakespeare, Homer, Dante—are the reverse of Goethe in this respect. Their sensibility is of a fixed type, which we recognize whenever we mention their names, and their strength lies not, as with Goethe, in breaking it down or extending it, but in accepting and elaborating it, so that where they travel along, side by side with each other but not overlapping, Goethe travels transversely and in due course crosses their tracks. He did not encounter every poet, and of those he did encounter he was drawn to some more than to others, but in any ideal construction of his poetic mind we must look upon him as one who had it in him to enter into and become all poets, and thus to complete the extraordinary synthesis of poetic types which in his lifetime he came so near to completing.

It is, no doubt, a consequence of this changing sensibility that the reader of Goethe's poems finds himself again and again, even in spite of long familiarity, under the passing illusion that these poems are not the work of one author, but of many, as many, indeed, as there are poems or cycles of poems. The psychological fashion, the idiosyncrasy of one poem gives us no certain clue to the idiosyncrasy of the next; our whole training and experience in poetry leads us to expect the idiosyncrasy to reveal itself quickly, and to repeat itself, and it is only with difficulty that we adjust our minds to a poet who habitually thwarts this expectation and compels us to begin each new poem—or, as the case may be, each group of poems or each section of a poem—as if we were beginning a new author.

The lines entitled "Auf dem See" are peculiarly valuable, because here, for once, we can detect a change of sensibility within the limits of a short poem. The poem belongs to the year 1775; Goethe is in Switzerland, trying to forget Lili Schönemann; the immediate occasion is a holiday excursion on Lake Zürich. "I draw new nourishment and new blood from the open world about me. Nature, who holds me to her bosom, is so kind and good. The waves rock our boat upwards to the oar-beats, and the mountains, clouded above, meet us in our course":

> Und frische Nahrung, neues Blut
> Saug' ich aus freier Welt;
> Wie ist Natur so hold und gut,
> Die mich am Busen hält!
> Die Welle wieget unsern Kahn
> Im Rudertakt hinauf,
> Und Berge, wolkig himmelan,
> Begegnen unserm Lauf.

Notice the reliance on groping, nestling, Werther-like imagery—motherhood, nourishment, and the blind flowing of the blood — coupled with the curious unsteadiness of the outer world, the lake tilted upwards towards the distant mountains, the mountains advancing to meet the boat. It is a mood which threatens at any moment to lose its visual grasp on things, and to pass into pure introspection; the external world is dissolving, the eyes are closing. The poem pauses here, and resumes immediately at the point at which this incipient day-dream is broken, "Why do my eyes droop? Golden dreams, do you return? Away, thou dream, for all thy gold. Here too there is life and love":

> Aug', mein Aug', was sinkst du nieder?
> Goldne Träume, kommt ihr wieder?
> Weg, du Traum, so gold du bist:
> Hier auch Lieb' und Leben ist,

and it concludes with a third stanza which balances the first and, like it, interprets the surrounding landscape, but with the change of rhythm and mood announced by this transitional middle passage. The poet flings off the sentimental retrospect which has crept upon him unawares and concentrates resolutely on the visible world. He sees clearly now and accurately, and with growing solidity of vision: "On the waters a thousand stars hover and twinkle, soft clouds drink up the towering distance round about, the morning breeze wings round the shady bay, and the ripening fruit is mirrored in the lake":

> Auf der Welle blinken
> Tausend schwebende Sterne,
> Weiche Nebel trinken
> Rings die türmende Ferne;
> Morgenwind umflügelt
> Die beschattete Bucht,
> Und im See bespiegelt
> Sich die reifende Frucht.

This is a shift of consciousness which can be better
described in terms of all the arts than in terms of the
poetic art only.   It takes us from vague feeling to sharp
seeing, from dreaminess to reality, from atmosphere to
coherence, and it may serve to remind us that the
affinities of Goethe's consciousness are almost as strong
in the non-literary field as in the literary.   Not that he
was an artist or a musician, or that his taste in either
field was infallible.   In music he was more at home with
his friend Zelter than with Beethoven; his feeling for
painting seems unduly literary now, and if we possessed
nothing of his but his drawings we should not remember
him.   On the other hand, we have only to consider the
essentially musical form of *Faust* or *Torquato Tasso*,
the splendidly visual and plastic qualities of such poems
as the "Song of the Fates" from *Iphigenie auf Tauris*
or the idyll of "Alexis und Dora," and the presence of
these qualities pervasively and unobtrusively in all
Goethe's verses to recognize the force of H. S. Chamber-
lain's contention—argued suggestively and at length in
his *Goethe*—that here is a poetic mind in which the
sensibilities that pertain to the sister arts of painting,
sculpture, music are all present and contributory to
the central poetic activity, not in the way of influences
operating from without — a common phenomenon in
modern poetry — but as constituent and essential
elements operating instinctively.   In this light Goethe's
long training as a draughtsman, dating from Frankfurt
days and lasting till his Italian journey and after, and
his long interest in problems of opera—not at first
sight fruitful or effective pursuits—may be regarded as
important indications of the complex æsthetic life within
him, and as activities which were somehow necessary
to it, either for discipline or release.   We arrive finally
at the conception of a mind endowed with such inner
versatility that it possesses the key to all the arts and
all the sensibilities, yet at the same time is compelled

to pour its secrets into literature only. Goethe, we might say, is at once a universal artist and a pure poet. All the arts are in him, yet the one art, the art of poetry, presides over the others and turns them to its own ends. A speculative interpretation, no doubt, yet helpful in explaining a poetic genius at once highly visual, yet rarely pictorial; richly musical in sound and still more so in structure, yet not usually studious of musical effects; plastic always, yet never obviously so, never Parnassian.

It is not to be wondered that a poet of this wide-ranging sensibility should often seem by comparison with other poets to lack suitable subjects, and even to lack a field of his own. *Faust* notwithstanding, Goethe is unlike the great epic writers who were able to devote their life-energy to a given fable, or a given region of life. It was only because the Faust theme was so accommodating that he was able to stay with it, and it never held him steadfastly as the fall of man held Milton, or as the founding of Rome held Virgil. Compared with them, Goethe is indeed a poet without a theme. Yet if he found it harder than they to let himself go in a chosen subject, it was not for any lack of contact with the outer world, or with anything outside him. It was rather that he had too much contact; his contact was too many-sided, too complete, too philosophical to allow itself to be narrowed or easily satisfied by particular plots or particular characters. How immense his range of passionate interest was is finely indicated by a passage from his essay "On Granite," written after a visit to the Harz mountains. "I do not fear the reproach," he says, "that it is some spirit of contradiction in me that has led me from the contemplation and delineation of the human heart, the youngest, the most varied, the most unstable, the most fickle, the most fragile part of creation, to the consideration of the oldest, the firmest, the deepest, the most unshakable of the sons of nature. For it will be granted that all

natural things are in exact correspondence, and that the
inquiring spirit is not willing to be shut off from anything
within its reach.   Besides, I have suffered and still
suffer so much from the shiftings of the human mood
and its quick motions in myself and others, that perhaps
I am entitled to the sublime repose which comes in this
mute and solitary closeness to Nature quietly whispering
in her grandeur.   Let those who have a feeling for this
do as I do."

Obviously, there is a close correspondence between
this scale of phenomena in the outer world and the scale
of sensibilities which we have discovered in Goethe; it
was inevitable that the one should seek and find the
other.   And this very quickly happened.   No sooner
was Goethe set free from the routine of home than his
mind and senses began to wander up and down the
keyboard of life, and to try the notes at top and bottom.
In contrast with the humanistic education which he
had received at his father's hands, we find him in
university years stealing time from the law courses to
which he was committed, and from the study of poetry
which he could not repress, to improve himself seriously
as an artist, and to indulge his interest in physiology
and anatomy by frequenting the laboratories and the
society of his medical confrères.   This was no caprice.
In thus spreading himself over a variety of studies,
which seem at first to be widely separated and even
divergent, he was not playing the dilettante, he was
establishing important points in the route which he was
destined to travel back and forth to the end of his days.
It was not a question of venting the impulses of
sporadic genius, or of academic curiosity, but of finding
as quickly as possible in the outer world the wide
domain in which his unlimited perceptiveness could
spend itself.   If we at first miss the sense of direction
in these distributed interests and are perplexed by
them, this is simply another aspect of the perplexity

which we experience when we first encounter his changes
of sensibility.   The line which joins them lies across
the line which our minds, prompted by our knowledge
of other poets, have probably drawn in anticipation.
In adding physiology—and later geology, botany, optics
—to art and letters, Goethe was moving as consistently
in his æsthetic world as Wordsworth when he crossed
the hills from one lake to another, or Shakespeare when
he turned from Plutarch to Holinshed or from the
tragedy of jealousy to the tragedy of ambition.

It is unlikely that Goethe realized this fully at so early
a date.   Full realization of it can scarcely have dawned
on him before his visit to Italy.   But it is hard to
believe that there was not some partial realization before
then.   In deciding to go to Weimar in 1775 he was
making exactly the choice that his genius required.   In
Weimar he reached the scale of things more intimately
and at a greater number of points than would have been
possible if he had roamed up and down Europe like
Byron, or travelled to far continents like Alexander von
Humboldt.   Here he touched the top and bottom of
human society; noble and peasant played on him alike.
He holidayed with his ruler and brooded over his
excesses, he asked also upon a time how he should write
his *Iphigenie auf Tauris* when the weavers of Apolda
were starving.   Here we see how in this Weimar duchy
the human part of the scale thrust itself on him.   And
the rest is behind and beneath—the forests, the hills,
and the rivers of Thuringia, all intimately his and
calling for his attention.   He makes roads, plants trees,
administers mines, and touches Nature in countless
other active ways that would never have been opened to
him in the world at large.   Here, like the ancient
Greeks, he had the great world in small, and this was
what he wanted.   If he had not gone to Weimar or to
some place like it he would in all probability have lost
his grasp and become a poet more like other poets,

instead of the unique poet he was. Instead of ranging the cross-section of natural life—the scale of being climbing from low to high, and then again from high to low—he would have become a poet of limited style and sensibility, repeating and extending his early successes. He would have followed up *Götz von Berlichingen* and become a sort of Scott, or he would have followed up *Werther* and become a sort of Chateaubriand. In the deeper sense that it gave him a working horizon for his multiple apprehensions, it was Weimar that made him; and it was in his early years in Weimar that he wrote the essay "On Granite," in which he seems to announce his recognition of his true field of activity.

This field of activity would have been more quickly apparent in Goethe's verses if he had described and interpreted it explicitly in some poetic treatise on nature, some modern *De Rerum Natura*. He wrote no such treatise, though he contemplated one and there are indications that he might have succeeded. His two short poems in Lucretian style on the metamorphosis of plants and animals read almost like extracts from it. More especially his felicitous treatment of plant-life raises the question whether it was not in his power to write poetry of this order on a more extended scale and to compose his natural philosophy into an epic, but the evidence is too slight to be conclusive. In the Classical Walpurgisnacht of *Faust* he hints again, though in a quite different vein, at what he might have made of a vast nature-theme. There is nothing Lucretian here, the old poet seems at play rather than at work, he does as he pleases. Yet there arises from this singular composition a fascinating picture of the early world and of the world in the making. In this oddest of poetic adventures the play of natural forces, of earthquake, fire, and flood, the slime and decay of lower organisms, the animal monstrosities of the remote past, the reedy rivers, the ozone of the seashore pass imperceptibly into the life of myths and heroes—the sphinxes, the centaurs, the sirens, the Argonauts, Hercules, Helena—and the modern scientist and the ancient philosopher wander through it all and argue its meaning. It is in this mythical vein rather than in the Lucretian that Goethe might conceivably have written his scientific poem.

But it will be clear from the brevity and the tentative nature of these portions of his verse that, whatever he might conceivably have done, it was not his way to extend himself in the poetry of rocks, and stones, and trees. It is not by any direct rendering of outer nature and the physical structure of the world that he stands as a poet of nature. Indeed the descriptive powers upon which he would have been compelled to draw in such an endeavour are as conspicuous for the sparing use he preferred to make of them as for their magnificence when their chance came; in spite of Faust's Easter Sunday walk and the first Walpurgisnacht we should never call him a landscape poet, or imagine him courting the epithet. So foreign was all topography to him as a poet that we shall search his verses almost in vain for descriptive pieces, though at the cooler level of prose we shall find some distinguished items, such as the description of Mont Blanc as Goethe saw it on his second visit to Switzerland, or the Sesenheim landscape as he remembered it in later years.

What is true of landscape description is true of all aspects of the non-human world—Goethe is seldom able to turn them directly to poetic account, and never able to rely on them for long. If we look more closely at his poem on the metamorphosis of plants we find that it is far from being the exclusively botanical poem that it seems to be at first glance. True, Goethe printed it in his botanical writings, but he nevertheless wrote it primarily for Christiane Vulpius, and it is she whom he addresses throughout. Having put before her his verbal

diagrams of plant life—seed, leaf, flower, fruit—he
concludes with the human analogy and reminds her
that the growth of their relationship from its beginning
to their present love and union is identical with the
plant-growth she has just witnessed. "Remember, too,
how from the seed of acquaintance the sweet wont
gradually sprouted in us, how friendship powerfully
came from within, and how love at last begot the flowers
and the fruits":

> O, gedenke denn auch, wie aus dem Keim der Bekanntschaft
> Nach und nach in uns holde Gewohnheit entspross,
> Freundschaft sich mit Macht aus unserm Innern enthüllte,
> Und wie Amor zuletzt Blüten und Früchte gezeugt.

Philosophical reasons apart, it is typical of him as a
poet that his would-be botanical lines should border
on the erotic and that even here the human note should
force its way to the front of his mind. What in any
other nature poet would be landscape poetry, nature
description, nature myth, or the poetry of birds, beasts,
and flowers, is represented in Goethe's work almost
exclusively by his scientific writings. When he turned
his attention specifically to the life of organic and
inorganic nature, as opposed to the life of man, he did
not usually discover in himself the urgent functional
need which we have recognized as the prime motive of
his poetry, and there are probably less than half a dozen
instances in his career when he consented to write poetry
under such conditions. It was the scientific impulse
that was habitually quickened—an impulse closely
related to his poetic impulse, but not identical with it,
as the results show. For one solitary meteorological
poem—celebrating the work of Howard who introduced
the current terminology for describing cloud-forms—
we have several meteorological papers; and we have
only to put this solitary poem beside the cloud-poetry
of Wordsworth or the occasional cloud-imagery in other

poems of Goethe's to see that it is primarily an attempt
to put scientific and philosophical thoughts into metre
and is only nominally a poem.   As in the case of the
metamorphosis pieces we do not feel the compelling
creative impulse which we expect to feel when we take
up a poem of Goethe's.   There is only one exception.
It is a poem describing the death of a fly.   "Greedily
it sucks up the poison and never stops, seduced by the
first sip.   It suspects nothing, yet its delicate leg-joints
are paralysed already.   No longer skilled to clean its
wings or trim its head, its life loses itself in indulgence.
Its feet barely support it, and thus it drinks and drinks,
till in the midst of drinking death beclouds its thousand
eyes ":

> Sie saugt mit Gier verrätrisches Getränke
> Unabgesetzt, vom ersten Zug verführt;
> Sie fühlt sich wohl, und längst sind die Gelenke
> Der zarten Beinchen schon paralysiert:
> Nicht mehr gewandt, die Flügelchen zu putzen,
> Nicht mehr geschickt, das Köpfchen aufzustutzen—
> Das Leben so sich im Genuss verliert.
> Zum Stehen kaum wird noch das Füsschen taugen;
> So schlürft sie fort, und mitten unterm Saugen
> Umnebelt ihr der Tod die tausend Augen.

Here there can be no question.   This is as convincing
an essay in scientific naturalism as we shall find in
poetry, and the last line is masterly.   No doubt the
human reference can be felt by those who know Goethe.
We remember Faust's outcry to Mephistopheles: "If
you can deceive me with delight" (Kannst du mich
mit Genuss betrügen), and we remember the watch-
man's song on his tower and Goethe's inexhaustible
joy in the play of light on the visible world.   If we
transfer these observations of the poisoned fly to the
human plane we feel at once how Goethean they are,
how peculiarly fitted Goethe was to shudder at this
sensual self-betrayal and this fearful darkening of
the sight.   Yet he stands aloof and scientific to the

end and leaves his remorseless observations to speak
for themselves.

This is an isolated poem, there is no other like it in all
Goethe.   It is only when he turns to himself and to his
kind that he is able to give full and easy vent to his
nature feeling.   Give him the necessary impetus to
write or refashion a love-poem, and he will pour all
nature into it, making the rhythm of the body as the
rhythm of the stars.   "When you move in the dance,
all the constellations move with you and about you":

> Wenn du im Tanze dich regst
> So regen sich alle Gestirne
> Mit dir und um dich umher.

Ask him to characterize the human soul, and he thinks
of the mountain cascade and the wind on the lake.
"The soul of man is like water, it comes from heaven
and mounts to heaven and must return to earth in
eternal change.   The clear water streams from the high
cliff, then scatters sweetly in cloudy waves till it reaches
the level rock; where, veiling and rustling, it wanders
down.   If crags meet it in its fall it foams angrily into
the abyss.   In its shallow bed it creeps along the
meadowy vale, and in the smooth lake all the constellations feast themselves.   Wind is the lover of the waters,
wind mixes the foaming waves from within.   Soul of
man, how art thou like to water; fate of man, how art
thou like to wind":

> Des Menschen Seele,
> Gleicht dem Wasser:
> Vom Himmel kommt es,
> Zum Himmel steigt es,
> Und wieder nieder
> Zur Erde muss es,
> Ewig wechselnd.
>
> Strömt von der hohen
> Steilen Felswand
> Der reine Strahl,
> Dann stäubt er lieblich

In Wolkenwellen
Zum glatten Fels,
Und leicht empfangen
Wallt er verschleiernd,
Leisrauschend
Zur Tiefe nieder.

Ragen Klippen
Dem Sturz entgegen,
Schäumt er unmutig
Stufenweise
Zum Abgrund.

Im flachen Bette
Schleicht er das Wiesental hin,
Und in dem glatten See
Weiden ihr Antlitz
Alle Gestirne.

Wind ist der Welle
Lieblicher Buhler;
Wind mischt vom Grund aus
Schäumende Wogen.

Seele des Menschen,
Wie gleichst du dem Wasser!
Schicksal des Menschen,
Wie gleichst du dem Wind!

Let the death of a young friend cut him to the quick and
he will cry out to nature in his grief and evoke the
stable rocks and the ever-flowing waters, the years
and the changes of the seasons: "Nature, how sure and
great thou art in all things! Heaven and earth follow
everlasting laws. Years follow years, summer gives its
hand to spring and winter to autumn. The rocks stand
firm, the eternal water foams down roaring from the
cloudy chasm":

Ach, Natur, wie sicher und gross in allem erscheinst du!
   Himmel und Erde befolgt ewiges, festes Gesetz.
Jahre folgen auf Jahre, dem Frühlinge reichet der Sommer,
   Und dem reichlichen Herbst traulich der Winter die Hand.
Felsen stehen gegründet, es stürzt sich das ewige Wasser
   Aus der bewölkten Kluft schäumend und brausend hinab.

N

Goethe's verse is full of these things. *Faust*, the all-too-human—a legend more of the study than of the open air when he took it up—is drenched in nature by the time he has finished with it from the stormy radiance of the archangels' inaugural song and the fugitive snows of the early Eastertide to the blue sky and the wisps of cloud which usher the poem out.

This is Goethe's way. With the full scale of the natural world constantly, vividly, actively before him, he is as dependent on humanity for poetic inspiration as either Pope or Shakespeare. The conditions under which he elected to live bear witness to it. From first to last he was a town-dweller; when he went to the woods or to the mountains the chances were that he did not go unaccompanied; his happiest holidays were spent in crowded watering-places; he never deserted his kind for long. Deprived of closer human relationships he might still have discovered the intermaxillary bone and the leaf-morphology of plants, but there would have been no *Faust*, no "Erlkönig," no poetry of the moon and the waters. There might have been no poetry at all. But this is rank speculation. He could not have lived under such conditions.

Moreover, there is no trace in Goethe's poetry of the dwarfing and restricting of the human consciousness which we might expect to follow from his habitual placing of it in the natural scale. The smothering of man in a jungle of leafage, or the crushing of him in the jaws of casualty, has no place in his pages. His sense of environment is so unconfined, so little bounded by time or locality, that we cannot conveniently call it by this name, though it is the right name. In his world the mind of man ranges less imperiously, it may be, than in Shakespeare's—though we have the great instance of *Faust* to give us pause—but not less freely. Even his sense of history is never thwarted by his sense of nature. The varieties of human experience, he seems to say,

must be sought in all the centuries, and there is nothing
in the records of human life long past that cannot by
vivid re-experience find its place in the living present
and become once more a function of the passing moment.
And in this sense, never relinquishing his hold on nature,
never antiquarian, Goethe ranges the remote ages of
man and adds their treasures to the treasures of the
world about him.

There is no better instance of the blending of past
and present, of history and nature, in Goethe's poetry,
than the fifteenth of the *Roman Elegies*, in which he
describes himself sitting in a Roman inn waiting for his
amorous rendezvous at the fourth hour after sundown.
Sitting there in musing impatience, he goes back in
thought to the beginnings of Rome, its rise and fall
and rise again, ever gilded by this sun which he bids
hasten to set its fires on the domes and obelisks and
plunge into the sea in order that the moment he desires
may come the quicker. "Plunge into the sea so that
to-morrow you may behold the sooner what has given
you divine pleasure for centuries. These damp and
reedy shores, these hills with their dark growth of trees,
showed only a few huts at first, then you suddenly saw
them alive with a throng of fortunate brigands. All
that there was they brought to this one place. The
rest of the round world was scarcely worth your gaze.
Here you saw a world arise and crumble, and on the
ruins you saw another and even a greater world arise.
May the Fates spin my thread cunningly and slowly
that I may long see this place with your light on it.
But now let the happy hour come. Do I hear it
already?"

Stürze dich eilig ins Meer, um morgen früher zu sehen,
  Was Jahrhunderte schon göttliche Lust dir gewährt:
Diese feuchten, mit Rohr so lange bewachsnen Gestade,
  Diese mit Bäumen und Busch düster beschatteten Höhn.
Wenig Hütten zeigten sie erst; dann sahst du auf einmal
  Sie vom wimmelnden Volk glücklicher Räuber belebt.

Alles schleppten sie drauf an diese Stätte zusammen;
    Kaum war das übrige Rund deiner Betrachtung noch wert.
Sahst eine Welt hier entstehn, sahst dann eine Welt hier in Trümmern,
    Aus den Trümmern aufs neu' fast eine grössere Welt!
Dass ich diese noch lange von dir beleuchtet erblicke,
    Spinne die Parze mir klug langsam den Faden herab.
Aber sie eile herbei, die schön bezeichnete Stunde!—
    Glücklich! hör' ich sie schon?

Yet, for all his historical vision, it is in the interpretation of immediate life and of himself that Goethe
excels and it is here that we must look for his most daring
successes. Characteristically enough, his knowledge of
history, far from hampering him in this, seems rather to
assist him, giving him a greater knowledge of himself, a
completer self-consciousness than he could have achieved
without it. The scenes and figures which he takes from
tradition do not so much draw him back into their past
as move forward into his present and serve his lyrical
purpose, as they do in this Roman Elegy. But there
are richer examples. Goethe's self-knowledge at the
time of writing *Torquato Tasso* is all the greater for his
contact with Renaissance thought. By drawing on
Tasso and Tasso's world he saw himself much more
clearly and explicitly than if, shrinking from the historical past in an access of Rousseauism, he had sought
some contemporary fable, or perhaps avoided fable
altogether. In this poem the usual historical process is
reversed; it is not the eighteenth century interpreting
the sixteenth, but conversely the sixteenth interpreting
the eighteenth. By turning to Tasso and his century
at the right moment Goethe was instinctively choosing
the tools he needed for his poetic self-analysis.

Thus neither the dominant scale of natural things,
ranging from the stablest of the rocks to the quivering
thoughts of modern man, nor the vast historical perspective which he found it so easy to reconcile with it,
in any way detracts from his emphasis on the living
consciousness, and on the need of laying it bare and of

adventuring in it to the limit. Imbued as he was at all times with the sense of unconscious life about him and within him, he nevertheless probes his consciousness —using all the resources of poetry for the purpose— with a skill and a thoroughness which were new in literature.

The highest pitch of this self-realization in Goethe's poetry, the farthest mark in his extension upwards of the scale of being, is registered in the closing act of *Faust*. The kind of self-projection which he had made years before by breaking himself up into Tasso, Antonio, and others—as if the Tasso story were a prism through which he passed the undifferentiated white light of himself so as to read it in many-coloured spectral analysis —reaches its greatest complexity here. In order to achieve this most elaborate and thorough-going unearthing of himself at the close—or, for the older portions of the text, in anticipation of the close—of a crowded life he takes whatever implements he can find in the heaped pillage of the ages which—like the booty that Mephistopheles brings home from the high seas and spreads before his master—lies now at his august disposal. It matters not whence they hail. Be they echoes of Ovid or echoes of Dante, figures from a German fairy-tale or from a Renaissance canvas, they are all grist to his mill. The poetic accents may shift from Shakespeare to Swedenborg, the outer setting from Ruysdael to Raphael, the common intention remains. Every detail, ancient or modern, in this extraordinary medley serves the deeper purpose of mapping out the less accessible regions of Goethe's mind and giving them contour and definition.

The episode of Philemon and Baucis, whose plot of land with its lime-trees, its crumbling chapel, and its view of the sea lies tauntingly under Faust's nose, until with the help of his desperate henchmen he ruthlessly appropriates it—the old couple die of shock, and Faust must share the guilt—does not stir us deeply as narrative; it is tritely told, its intrinsic beauties are not conspicuous. Yet no sooner has it been read and experienced than it assumes a mental value quite out of proportion to its external appeal. It is not merely that it identifies itself with all that goes by the name of hearth and home and discovers whatever there is of natural piety in those who read it. Other works of poetry do this not less skilfully. But there is probably no other piece of poetry which sets these rooted associations in such a long perspective and so successfully renders the disturbing memory of them lingering in a mind no longer young. By some strange cunning which we cannot explain, we are made to see this aged pair, their peace, their destruction, down a great vista of time, and yet to see it closely, as if the tragedy were something that happened long ago and is also happening now. We know what this means. It is in Goethe's mind that Philemon and Baucis are both past and present, and the region of his mind which they inhabit is that in which his oldest personal associations are kept.

No doubt the episode serves other purposes—there are dramatic purposes, both obvious and elusive—but this one goes deepest. Only when we recognize that Goethe is clearing himself of his obscurer relations to the old order of things, emptying one of the dustiest cupboards of his mind in a last house-cleaning, can we appreciate the finer points of this anecdote and assure ourselves that behind its artlessness there is art of a rare order—art which knows how to strike home to the inner mind and establish its uncanny references there with a minimum of effort and delay. How else should we account for the defencelessness of Faust's outcry at the sound of the chapel-bell, as also for the poignancy and the ghostliness of it? "This cursed ringing, it wounds me intolerably like a treacherous shot. Before my eyes my kingdom is infinite, but vexation teases me from behind, reminding me with envious noise that my

great possessions are impure. The lime-tree grove, the
brown cottage, the crumbling chapel are not mine.
If I wished to stroll there I should shudder at strange
shadows. This is a thorn to the sight and a thorn to
the feet. Would that I were far from here ":

> Verdammtes Läuten! Allzuschändlich
> Verwundet's, wie ein tückischer Schuss;
> Vor Augen ist mein Reich unendlich,
> Im Rücken neckt mich der Verdruss,
> Erinnert mich durch neidische Laute:
> Mein Hochbesitz, er ist nicht rein,
> Der Lindenraum, die braune Baute,
> Das morsche Kirchlein ist nicht mein.
> Und wünscht' ich, dort mich zu erholen,
> Vor fremdem Schatten schaudert mir,
> Ist Dorn den Augen, Dorn den Sohlen;
> O! wär' ich weit hinweg von hier!

These are accents which drama cannot account for.
Why does Faust feel that he is being attacked from
behind? Why does he say that his possessions are not
pure, when he might have said not complete? Why
this exasperated shrinking from shadows? Dramatically Faust has only to raise his finger and the troublesome tenants will go. But it is the something behind,
of which they are the symbol, that haunts him and—
even at the end and summit of life—wrings these accents
of torture from him. Nowhere in Faust is the psychological interpretation more expressly called for. And
remembering that the characters of Faust are all limbs
of one body, phases of one mind, we shall not be pressing
the interpretation too far if we see in the wanderer who
returns after long absence to express his gratitude to
the aged couple the voice of Goethe's simpler piety—
was not Goethe styled the "wanderer" in his Wetzlar
days?—and in Faust, the partner of Mephistopheles,
the voice of its tragic irreconcilableness with sovereign
life. It is as if Goethe had dug something out of himself
at a lower stratum of his consciousness than he was

usually able to reach. Now at the last he brings it to the surface, and in this way conquers it.

Finer in inspiration, and not less penetrating in its exploration of the subconscious mind, is Faust's encounter with the phantom of Care which immediately follows. It is Faust's last crisis on this side of the grave, and the phantom blinds him with her breath before she leaves him. There had been talk of Care earlier in the poem. This was in the First Part when Faust after his rebuff by the Earth-Spirit was sinking towards suicide, but the difference between this passage and the passage at the close is vital. In the first passage the poem talks about Care and recognizes some of her disguises, but in the second she appears in person and speaks directly for what she is. If it is possible to give immediate voice to the direr apprehensions that lie in wait, moment by moment, at the back of every human mind—those ever-present fears of the lurking stagnation and paralysis that threaten to corrode the well-directed life and bring it to naught—if it is possible to drag all this out into the conscious daylight and be rid of it, Goethe does it here in this masterly passage. Seldom, if ever, had he sent such a shaft of light into himself, or lit up so deep a recess. "Shall he go or shall he come? All resolve is taken from him. In the middle of the trodden road he stumbles and feels his way. He loses himself farther and farther, sees things more and more awry; a burden to himself and others; panting, choking; lifeless, yet breathing still; neither despairing nor yielding. So he drifts and cannot stop, gives up with pain, obeys with revulsion; now free, now crushed; now drowsed, now weakly refreshed. All this holds him where he is, and prepares him for hell":

> Soll er gehen, soll er kommen?
> Der Entschluss ist ihm genommen;
> Auf gebahnten Weges Mitte
> Wankt er tastend halbe Schritte.

Er verliert sich immer tiefer,
Siehet alle Dinge schiefer,
Sich und andre lästig drückend,
Atem holend und erstickend;
Nicht erstickt und ohne Leben,
Nicht verzweifelnd, nicht ergeben.
So ein unaufhaltsam Rollen,
Schmerzlich Lassen, widrig Sollen,
Bald Befreien, bald Erdrücken,
Halber Schlaf und schlecht Erquicken
Heftet ihn an seine Stelle
Und bereitet ihn zur Hölle.

Goethe had given Schiller a hint of this side of his nature when he admitted to him at the beginning of their closer acquaintance that there was in him "a certain darkness and hesitancy which he could never overcome" (eine Art Dunkelheit und Zaudern . . . über die ich nicht Herr werden kann). With the closing act of *Faust* before us we might say that he did overcome it when he extracted this poetic expression of it from the depths of himself and earned the right to say to his implacable enemy, "Thy stealthy power, O Care, I do not acknowledge":

Doch deine Macht, o Sorge, schleichend gross,
Ich werde sie nicht anerkennen.

These tragic elucidations of Goethe's darker self are only half of the picture. It is in this act of *Faust* that we must also look for his most radiant expression of confidence in the power of man, whether it be in this life or in some life to come. Having got rid of all that obscurely hampered or fettered him in his most private sense of the past and of his inner self, he can now adventure into the infinite future with a new serenity, exploring the beginnings of heavenly life so clear-sightedly that it seems that he is rather extending the bounds of mortality into the hereafter than overleaping them into some transcendent world. It is all one consciousness from first to last—from the faded stars, the night-wind, the mist and smoke of Faust's last evening on earth to the blue empyrean in which he soars triumphantly upwards to new states of being. The whole act is a unique landscape of Goethe's mind. We do not see everything that is there, but we see the extremities, the heights and the depths; and in what we see there is nothing dark, but all is flooded with intelligence and reason. The searchlight does not lie only on the summits, but the deepest caverns are known and illuminated.

It is in this sense that the close of *Faust* marks a climax. Nowhere else does Goethe probe his consciousness to such metaphysical depths, nowhere else does he carry his mental life so far beyond that of the sleeping rocks and the dreaming forests. Poetic explicitness, the exploring and the making conscious of the inner mind by means of poetry, could scarcely go farther than this. Yet even at this pitch the life of natural things is not forgotten, there is no break in the scale, the scale is simply lengthened at the upper end. It is not merely that we feel nature atmospherically everywhere in this poem. In his encounter with Care Faust cries out unequivocally that now he would be done with ghosts once for all, and that if he loses his hold on nature his ideal of humanity is gone. "Nature, if I could stand before thee a man alone, it would be worth while to be a man":

> Stünd' ich, Natur, vor dir ein Mann allein,
> Da wär's der Mühe wert, ein Mensch zu sein.

Besides, the deeper meaning of this third and last phase of his adventure with Mephistopheles—Gretchen was the first phase and Helena the second—turns wholly upon man's mastery of nature, as is clearly stated in that passage of suppressed vehemence in Act IV, in which Faust looks out over the ocean and desires to control and, as it were, to educate its turbulent and

senseless energy.   The ocean, says Faust in his Titanic
ambition, must be taught to bear itself like a man.   He
and the ocean are one and the same, and they must come
to terms with each other.   Thus anthropomorphically
he formulates his desire to master and harness it.   The
contest with lower nature—man's relation to it expressed
in the combative Faustian mode—is the central activity
of Faust's later years, and it is the motive power behind
the colonizing project which occupies him to the day of
his death.   At the end of *Faust* we are as near to the
elements as we were at the beginning, and we are just
as dependent on them for the meaning and the purpose
of life.

CHAPTER X

IT is not surprising that a poet of Goethe's sensibility should be slower to know himself and harder to follow at the start than other poets. For where they needed only to find their bent and keep to it, Goethe had to make the more arduous discovery that he was not a poet like them, that he had no bent of his own in their sense of the word, and that he would have to base his poetry on some new foundation if it was to stand secure. Until that foundation was established he was at the mercy of his unsuspected versatility and capable, as his work shows, of strange shifts of position. The shift from the unfinished *Egmont* or the *Urfaust*—MSS. which occupied him in 1775—to the prose draft of *Iphigenie auf Tauris*, made in Weimar four years later, or to the beginnings of *Torquato Tasso* which followed hard upon it is as striking as any in the annals of poetry, and no readers, however enlightened and alert, could have failed to be baffled by it.

But there is nothing enigmatic in it now. When Goethe allowed himself to take colour from Charlotte von Stein and to write as her temperament bade, he was obeying the same law of his nature as when in middle life he surrendered to Homer. The difference must be —for, granting that Charlotte stands not less than Homer for a way of poetry, there remains a palpable difference —that in the former case he was less sure of his ultimate line of movement; he was beginning or continuing his transverse journey without knowing it, and with a marked tendency to travel along instead of across; lacking any sure foothold as yet, he was more at the

nature, yet nothing is more certain than that he is unlike other poets of nature, unlike Wordsworth. Wordsworth, we should say offhand, has more nature in his poetry than Goethe and is therefore more a nature poet. But we do not understand Goethe until we have reversed this judgment. Wordsworth on further comparison proves to be a poet about nature. Save for a not wholly laudable substitution of natural diction for artificial, there is no evidence that the spirit of nature sinks much deeper into the stuff of Wordsworth's poetry than his argument takes it. He is called a nature poet chiefly because he talks about nature, describing it, interpreting it, revealing it; when he has delivered his nature message his nature poetry is complete. Unless we are students of Goethe this is what we mean by a nature poet, and we do not look for more from Wordsworth or any one. A nature poet is a poet who goes to nature for his themes.

Measured by this customary standard Goethe is an obvious misfit. As between man and nature he is, as we have seen, the poet of man. It is man, the moods and passions and dilemmas of man, that he is compelled to wait upon for poetic quickening, and there is no sure alternative. Put a lesser celandine before him and he will talk botany nine times out of ten. But in another sense—a sense so unforeseen that we can only learn it from him and would never have dreamed of it if he had not taught us—he is a nature poet and nothing else. The proof is this—that when we have become familiar enough with a sufficient area of his poetry to move freely in it and to begin to note its essential character, it is to nature that we must go for the only analogies that will help us to describe it. Many poets have written of the months and the seasons, and some have written nobly, but Goethe, who scarcely touches such topics, is the only poet to get the seasonal feeling everywhere into the life of his poetry so that not once or twice but continually, irrespective of when we read it or what the theme in

hand may be, we think of phases of the moon and the
ebb and flow of tides, of daffodils that come before the
swallow dares and of Indian summers bringing the late
growths, of recurrent periods of sun and bloom and of
the winter sleep that divides them each from each.
Witness those harbingers of a pagan summer which come
and go like swallows in the half-virginal love-poetry to
Charlotte—poems like "Der Becher" and "Nachtge-
danken," which bring hints of the warm South with
them and tell of the halcyon days that will come with
the ripeness of time. "Unhappy stars, I pity you, in
your resplendent beauty, you who give light to the
stormbeat sailor, unrewarded of gods and men. For
you know not love, and never have known it. Unceas-
ingly the eternal hours lead you in ranks across the
spacious heavens. What a journey you have made,
while I linger here in the arms of my loved one, forgetful
of you and of the midnight!"

> Euch bedaur' ich, unglücksel'ge Sterne,
> Die ihr schön seid und so herrlich scheinet,
> Dem bedrängten Schiffer gerne leuchtet,
> Unbelohnt von Göttern und von Menschen:
> Denn ihr liebt nicht, kanntet nie die Liebe!
> Unaufhaltsam führen ew'ge Stunden
> Eure Reihen durch den weiten Himmel.
> Welche Reise habt ihr schon vollendet,
> Seit ich, weilend in dem Arm der Liebsten,
> Euer und der Mitternacht vergessen!

This, written in or about 1781, with *Torquato Tasso*
unfinished and the dominion of Charlotte outwardly
unshaken, is as mysteriously eloquent as the first crocuses
and, if we know Goethe well, it says exactly what they say.

This is Goethe's triumph, that he writes in such con-
formity with Nature that she lends him her ways and
her habits to shape his world with. All the disadvantages he is at when we approach him conventionally
—his looseness of composition, his flat endings, his
fragmentariness, his lack of dispatch—turn to crowning

virtues when seen in their true perspective. It was not because of any inexpertness that Goethe was so little effective as a dramatist—he showed more than once that he had all the dramatic technique that was needed —it was rather because his terminal sense, his sense of climax and extremity, of strong beginnings and strong endings, without which there can be no true drama, was incompatible with his deeper sense of life unterminated, life which, like the life of nature, never begins and never ends, but moves in an eternal ever-changing present. For it is man, not nature, who is the dramatist. How was Goethe to write dramatically of great dooms and destinies when he had as little catastrophic sense of these things as the wind in the trees? If instead of following his instincts he had forced them and wrung dramatic crises from himself, he would have forfeited his birthright.

His defective feeling for tragedy—his reluctance to write it and his frequent lack of finish when he wrote it —has often been commented on, and there is no doubt about it. The least real act in *Werther* is the act of suicide that ends it; *Torquato Tasso* is tragic in its issues, but not in fact; Gretchen passes in the dark and so does Egmont. And in the close of *Faust* where, as elsewhere in this poem, Goethe is drawn a little farther than he readily chooses to go and is compelled to face the fact of death, physical death, and speak his mind on it, what has he to say? So ineloquent is he on the ageless theme of mortality and the dust we come to— the glory of many poets and especially of Shakespeare —that he frankly borrows an Elizabethan gravediggers' catch to stop the inconvenient gap and adds next to nothing of his own. The struggle for Faust's soul, fought out between the angels and the devils over his prone corpse, is so far from equalling the great scenes that precede and follow it—so uncomfortable in its humour, so obviously decorative, so lengthy in view of the little

o

it has to say—that we must suspect a desire on Goethe's part to cover up an embarrassing problem which he had hitherto managed to avoid; for he has much the same blind spot in him as his hero, who, failing to know death when it came, mistook the gravediggers for his employees in the work of life.

This is the negative side of the picture. Against it we must set the great positive achievement. The sense of unquenchable and indestructible life which Goethe conveys in these scenes, when read in sequence, is perhaps without rival in literature. Other poets have ventured into the hereafter, but none has quite so successfully carried over into it the vital qualities of earthly existence—the enterprise, the challenge, the limitless future, that call out the adventurer in man and drive him towards incredible goals. In the death-scene of *Faust* there is nothing so unreal as the death, Faust's energy seeming to grow gigantically in his last moments; nothing so certain as the certainty that life immediate is life eternal. The phantom of death which few poets would have refrained from introducing is hinted at, but not shown. Care may be Death's ally, but she is not Death. She is a spectre of Life, the dark side of the Faustian restlessness, the parasite of the daily world and the living present. Even in these fundamentals of life and death Goethe is like nature. He is so close to the process of nature, so wholly possessed by the sense of continuance, by the mingling of change and perman-ence, energy and stagnation in the passing moment, that he can speak of nothing else, and death, decay, corruption leave him mute. Only through the ironical mouthpiece of Mephistopheles can he talk of these things. We are tempted to say of him what he said of Hafiz: "It is your greatness that you cannot finish, it is your fate never to begin":

Dass du nicht enden kannst, das macht dich gross,
Und dass du nie beginnst, das ist dein Los.

By thus translating the life of a natural universe
into a universe of pure spirit Goethe proves as original
a poet in the long run as any of the great masters, whom
at one time or other he borrowed from or imitated.
If on first thoughts he seems to draw away from those
poets—Homer, Dante, Milton—whose work is based on
myth or doctrine, and to align himself with Shakespeare
as an essentially undogmatic mind, not circumscribed
by tradition or any ideal order of thought, this only
serves to mark another antithesis. For the qualities
in which it is appropriate that Goethe, the poet attuned
to nature, should be restrained or deficient are the very
qualities in which Shakespeare abounds. The opposition
is patent. Against the poet who cannot make an end
and whose world is immediate and perpetual we set the
poet for whom the wheel comes full circle and then stops
at his express bidding. There is no greater contrast
with the work of Goethe, in which, for example, the
poem of *Faust* is distributed everywhere, early, middle,
and late, and is incomplete at the last, than the great
cycle of Shakespeare's plays with its tragic climax and
its unique terminus, coming, not as with other poets,
because the message is delivered or the argument
expounded or the tale told, but because Shakespeare, the
imperious poet, chooses to stop.

There is no escaping the impression. If we come to
Shakespeare from Goethe we find that while Goethe
submits and allies himself to nature, Shakespeare with
his kingly mind confronts nature and dominates it;
Goethe is the functional, instinctive, unpractical poet,
writing—or not writing—because he cannot help it,
Shakespeare the voluntary poet, managing himself with
consummate generalship in every situation; Goethe is
the poet who learns, probes, watches, discovers, suffers
defeat, feels his way, Shakespeare the poet who stands
up valiantly against a turbulent universe and asserts
his Promethean mastery over it; Goethe is the man of

science who must explore his world with patience and self-subordination, Shakespeare the man of the Renaissance who in titanic self-reliance makes the world obey him and move at his command. Thus while Goethe's world is instinct with unconscious life and unconscious associations and only slowly and at the fag-end shows that the poet is beginning to "command" his poetry, Shakespeare's world luxuriates in consciousness and cares for nothing else. It is a world in which, as Goethe said in a late essay, no subliminal line is drawn, no secrets are kept. "Shakespeare," he writes, "associates himself with the world-spirit, like it he permeates the world, from neither is anything hid. But if it is the world-spirit's business to keep its secrets before and often after the deed, the poet's intent is to blab the secret, and to make us his confidants in the deed, if not before it. The criminal in authority, the good mind of little power, the abandoned in passion, the man of calm reflection, all wear their hearts on their sleeves, often contrary to all probability. Every one talks and gossips. Enough, the secret must out, though stones should tell it."

Nothing points more directly to the antithesis between Goethe's creative life and Shakespeare's — Goethe's creative life centred in nature, Shakespeare's centred in intellect; or—since it is a matter of purely mental processes in both cases—Goethe's creative life centred in the object of consciousness, Shakespeare's in the subject of consciousness. If Goethe shows what the high poetic mind, unhelped or unhindered by superstition, can create when it throws itself upon its feeling for outer things, Shakespeare shows what it can create when it relies on its inner powers. In this sense—a sense which has nothing to do with content—Shakespeare is the more subjective of the two.

Shakespeare's style accords perfectly with this subjective view of him. It is only by virtue of some subjective orientation that Shakespeare can associate himself so intimately with the words he uses—the words the mind of man invents and imposes on nature—and can delight and wanton metaphorically in them with such propriety. For in a sense quite peculiar to itself Shakespeare's world is a world of metaphor, living in metaphor and by metaphor, as if words and their winged associations were nature to it and all creation were verbal. There is no poet of the front rank who exults in his medium as Shakespeare does—we have to go to painters like Velazquez and Rubens for our nearest parallel—and there is no poet of any rank who identifies his medium so closely with his mental life, letting it assist his thought in the act of rendering it. Reading any inspired passage of Shakespeare—saving only those moments of utter simplicity which he shares with other poets—we seldom seem to pass through the words into any region beyond them to which they were the doors or the avenues, but they remain metaphorically active, changing shape and hue indefinitely, however far we plunge into them, and however well we know them. They never come to rest in their play of broken colour, they never release us from their infinite suggestiveness. Almost any page and any quotation will do:

> Hath oped his ponderous and marble jaws.

> Revisitest the glimpses of the moon.

No other poets, except those who have cultivated and sometimes over-cultivated the metaphorical tradition in English poetry, have attempted to write in this way. Goethe is as far from it as Dante. When Goethe said in early life that he was compelled to express himself figuratively (uneigentlich) but that he hoped ultimately to eliminate the figurative, he was anticipating the finer spirit and the finer necessity of his mature style, which is surpassingly lucid and direct and interposes the least possible verbal complexity between the mind that

reads his poems and the mind behind them.   His words
at their best have an easy transparency as of pools of
water so smooth that the eye sees into them before it
sees the surface of them—a natural limpidity not less
illustrious in its way than the firm clear words of Dante.
The lyric "Willkommen und Abschied," which, as we
have seen, sheds its load of metaphor and rises free of
it, most aptly symbolizes Goethe's ideal of style.   It is a
style as spontaneous as Shakespeare's, but it is the
opposite of Shakespeare's.

Of the Shakespearean style there seems to be only one
explanation—the alternative being to claim that no
explanation is possible.   If Shakespeare does not admit
us into any ideal realm beyond metaphor—any realm
in which words are quiescent, having done their work—
as Goethe frequently seems to do, and Dante and Homer
as well, it is because he has no ideal realm of this sort.
He shapes his world, it would seem, moment by moment,
trusting the powers that are in him and looking to no
others for support, and he shapes it with words, with
the life that he discovers in words and the life that words
discover in him.   Where other poets only interpret with
words, he lives with words and creates with words.   For
him verily the word is "in the beginning."   The word,
the might of the word, emanates from the heart of his
universe, and soars in metaphor to its farthest horizons.

This is not to deny Shakespeare his outwardness, or
to detract from it in any slightest degree.   No poet can
have touched the outer world at so many points, none
can have had so crowded an actuality to work on.   All
we are concerned with is his creative approach to this
actuality, his way of ordering it into poetry.   What
impresses us in Shakespeare—coming to him from
Goethe—is the greater disorder, not to say the complete
lack of order, of his outer world, and the single-handed
contest of his godlike intellect with it.   If there is a
formula for Shakespeare's creative life it must be in

these or in similar terms, suggestive of a poetic deity confronting a chaos. Only thus does the inevitability which we feel in the Shakespearean style become intelligible. Only thus—to take a further illustration—could it be appropriate for a poet to express his sense of order as Shakespeare seems inclined to express it—not pervasively, as something existent; or dogmatically, as something established; but inspirationally, as something struck off under high pressure from the dark anvil of his imagination, saying, not always with dramatic propriety, that life is thus and life is so. When Macbeth exclaims that life is a walking shadow, the colour of the thought may be his, but the impulse to express it is Shakespeare's, because all Shakespeare's characters have it. They all tend to blurt out their metaphysics in the heat of passion, and they can only have inherited this tendency from him.

Of such sort, we must infer, is Shakespeare's poetic mastery of the universe, and when the great moments are wiped out chaos is come again, as it came to Othello, to press ominously on the periphery of his vision. The nearer Shakespeare came to dominating this chaos, the freer he could be in letting us see it with him. It is at the two extremes of his career at the beginning and the end, that we are nearest to a managed and manipulated world—*Love's Labour's Lost* and *The Tempest*—and it is at the height of his power—*King Lear*—that we approach the expression of chaos. All other great poets, Goethe certainly, seem as they grow in power to move in the opposite direction, from disorder to order.

This—a Goethe look at Shakespeare—helps us not a little with Goethe. If it is possible, however tentatively, to question the existence of any enduring order in Shakespeare's world, it is not possible to question it in Goethe's. Not in any sudden fires of creation shooting their beams into the circumambient darkness does Goethe make his readings of the universe. The sense of some light, some order perceived or perceptible, in the outer world, in the world that is not himself, in nature, is always with him, and no Walpurgisnacht can deprive him of it; it is written large in the tone and texture of his poetry; on this score he is as unambiguous as either Milton or Dante. Yet no sooner have we admitted this than we have to discriminate again.

The distinction which we are able to draw in other poets between their sense of order—their ideas, their philosophy—and their poetry, as when we say that they build their poetry on their philosophy—their philosophy may be mythical as in Homer, theological as in Dante, scientific as in Lucretius—or that they introduce their philosophy into their poetry and make their poetry the vehicle of it, by theorizing or moralizing at convenient moments—this distinction collapses when we bring it to Goethe. Not that he is chary of philosophy. His wealth of moral and philosophical epigrams, rhymed and unrhymed, is such that if we possessed these only and the rest of his work were lost we should have to rank him with the greatest of men. But his philosophy is inseparable from his poetry in the sense that it is one with it, permeating it and permeated by it, present in it whether he formulates it or not, present in it whether he knows it or not.

Among the philosophical ideas by which he held most strongly in later life was the idea of polarity, the idea of the organic interdependence of opposites, of systole and diastole in all life-processes. In accordance with the common practice of poets Goethe both formulated this idea in prose and rendered it vividly in poetry, as in his lines in the *West-östlicher Divan* on breathing-in and breathing-out, the polarity of respiration. If this were all, Goethe's philosophical poetry would not be essentially different from any other. But when we look further we find that in noting these more conscious utterances we have only scratched the surface. The law of polarity was active in his poetry long before he had any sure thought of it, it was probably active in it from the beginning. Consider *Torquato Tasso*. What else is the interminable see-saw, the to and fro of attraction and repulsion between Tasso and Antonio, but the emergence of this law in lyrical drama? There can be no doubt about it. The idea of polarity fits the peculiar rhythm of *Torquato Tasso* as a hand fits a glove. Yet we can be reasonably certain that the idea of polarity was not clear to Goethe's mind during the writing of it, and we can be quite certain—the inner evidence, the feeling of the poem, is enough—that it had nothing to do with his conceiving or his shaping of it.

We may turn to any other of Goethe's dualisms—the two souls that wrestle in Faust's breast, Faust's elusive partnership with Mephistopheles, Prometheus and Epimetheus, the Brahmin and the pariah, the Faustian and non-Faustian modes, and much besides. This is not a set of variations on Dr. Jekyll and Mr. Hyde, or on any fixed cleavage of personality, for Goethe discovers it in outer nature—in gingko biloba, the Eastern tree with the split leaf—as readily as in himself. It is the law of polarity, operating unconsciously in Goethe's creative life and revealing itself to us in ways that he did not foresee. Taken together the poetic data are such that if Goethe had never formulated his belief in this law some patient reader would have extracted it sooner or later from the body of his writings and proved that it was part of him.

As far as we can see this holds good for the whole of Goethe's thought and admits of no exceptions. His ideas "grow" in his poetry, and we may extract them there much as we extract ideas from life. It is impossible to study *Faust* without pondering long and repeatedly on progress, perfectibility, evolution, the emergence of higher states from lower; the poem owes much of its immense prestige to its close association with these ideas;

everywhere in it there is a thrusting forward, a groping
from darkness to light, a spiral movement upwards, fitly
recalled in the conclusion by the Mater Gloriosa's words
to Gretchen, "Come, rise to higher spheres, if he feels
you are there he will follow":

> Komm! hebe dich zu höhern Sphären!
> Wenn er dich ahnet, folgt er nach.

This is the very life-breath of *Faust*, yet no thinking on
Goethe's part, no disquisitions on progress, no evolu-
tionary thesis could have made it so. Indeed, if Goethe
had succeeded in his intention of getting it off his hands
for good and all in 1790 it would have been a very
different work. The real mental character of the poem,
as it now stands, came to it rather in spite of Goethe's
deliberate intention than because of it. If the poem
fills us now with thoughts of growth and progress, that
is chiefly because it is itself a growth; the thoughts of
time, endeavour, fruition which it transmits to us
incessantly are in large measure its life-story, they are
the reflection in the texture of the poem of the time, the
endeavour, the fruition that went to the making of it.
Thus the natural configuration of the poem is an exact
clue to its mentality, its genesis—*mirabile dictu*—is
its philosophy.

The mutual interpenetration of poetry and ideas
can scarcely exceed this. Instead of the arbitrary
linking of the two which we commonly find, or the
arbitrary separation which some have vainly attempted,
or the partial identity, the overlapping of the one by the
other, which is the most we hope for, we discover in
Goethe, and perhaps in Goethe only, a complete identity,
the ideas residing in the poetry, like vital sap in a tree.
"Nature," he says, "has neither husk nor kernel, she is
everything at once":

> Natur hat weder Kern
> Noch Schale,
> Alles ist sie mit *einem* Male.

And what he says here of nature we must say of his poetry. Separating its ideas from its life is like peeling the onion, it is better not to begin. If at any point we suspect a discrepancy between the two, some artificial adjustment of thought to form, some encroachment of argument on spirit, the probability is that we do not know the poetry well enough. We study it further and the discrepancy goes.

Ethical thought or metaphysical thought—it makes no difference. Goethe's poetry would be ethical in every line if he had never indulged in an ethical maxim. Being the outcome of a functional exercise which awoke instinctively when his nature was disturbed, his poetry regularly turns upon these disturbances and involves us, whether we know it or not, in his way of dealing with them. If some poems moralize and others do not, this must not be misunderstood. The ethical values appear on the surface sometimes, but they are there always. We need not doubt that even such an ostensibly dramatic ballad as the "Erlkönig," where all is swift vivid portrayal and no interpretation is demanded, had its functional origin in Goethe's soul, that it corrected him tragically—on a smaller scale than *Werther*, but in *Werther's* sense—and that something of this corrective value lingers, often unrecognized, in the delight which it gives. It was not for nothing, it was not by any creative accident, that this crescendo of voices—voices of confidence, terror, and seduction—and this urgent impinging of the dream-world on the real shaped itself in the mind of the author of *Faust*, and, while in this case it might be hazardous to press the moral reading further, it would be idle to deny its legitimacy. If we cannot base it on the letter of the poem, we can base it on its subtler accents.

For a poet so constituted—committed in every syllable to the expression of his moral and metaphysical intuitions—there can be no divergence of poetry and truth. When Merck told Goethe in the seventeen-seventies that while other poets strove to give reality to their poetic dreams, his destiny was conversely to make reality poetic, he spoke with a prophet's insight. Goethe's poetry impresses us as being the clearest statement he could make of truth as he saw it, of the reality which he knew. If this had been the common reality poetry would have falsified it; but it was a different reality, a deeper reality; poetry alone could convey it accurately. How completely this deeper reality possessed and ruled him is well shown by his first recorded conversation with Schiller, in which he argued that the primal or Platonic form of plant-life which they were discussing was something that he had seen with his eyes, while Schiller, a better Kantian but a less extraordinary creature, stoutly maintained that this was impossible. Goethe did not argue further, but here and there in his late verses we can see this dilemma trembling on the verge of expression. His emotional conflict at the two Ulrikes, the one far away in Marienbad and the other ever-present, may be taken as a close corollary to his intellectual conflict with Schiller. "You spend your days by the hot springs, the thought perplexes me; for I hold you so wholly in my heart that I do not understand how you can be elsewhere":

> Am heissen Quell verbringst du deine Tage,
> Das regt mich auf zu innerm Zwist:
> Denn wie ich dich so ganz im Herzen trage,
> Begreif' ich nicht, wie du wo anders bist.

In a still later epigram, written probably in 1827, he touches—serenely now—on the same thought. "Now I know what a rose-bud is, now that the time of roses is past. A late-comer shines on its stem and, all alone, makes up the world of flowers":

> Nun weiss man erst, was Rosenknospe sei,
> Jetzt, da die Rosenzeit vorbei:

Ein Spätling noch am Stocke glänzt
Und ganz allein die Blumenwelt ergänzt.

Here in briefest compass is the ideal reality of Goethe's poetry: the tangible object in the outer world; the clear-eyed concentration on it, assisted here by the happy accident of its isolation in time and place; the seeing deeper into it, "Now I know what a rosebud is," he says; and the discovery in it of a realm of universals. There is no averting of the gaze, no forgetting, no fallacy. It is the "last rose of summer"—with what a difference!

Whether this ideal reality of Goethe's is the truth for others as well as for himself it is for others to say, though the wealth of nature analogy which comes unsolicited to the mind that communes with it is no uncertain token of its validity. Objective truth is not and can never be the criterion of poetry. Yet to Goethe's poetry the term "objective" clings, and with good reason. He, if any one, is the objective poet—not for the objective truth which he attained, but for the objective goal which he sought and the objective road which he trod. The pursuit of objective experience was his life's ruling passion, its be-all and end-all. Without it his concentration upon those moments in his life when self and nature were mysteriously made one in him again —his insistence, as it turned out, on registering in his poetry only what the whole of nature and the whole of himself could simultaneously corroborate—his inability to register anything short of that—would be capricious and meaningless. Questing his long life through for these experiences, losing them and recovering them again at some new height, ranging the field of history and science as few before him and none since, so as to understand them better and bring them nearer and nearer to his daily vision, and in this way approaching, though never possessing, that consummation of natural life which he called "the favour of the moment" (die Gunst des Augenblickes), and which he defined in the immortal

couplet, "Wherever you are, be all things as a child is.
Then you will *be* all things, and nothing can touch you":

> Nur wo du bist, sei alles, immer kindlich,
> So bist du alles, bist unüberwindlich,

he set down the quintessence of it when the impulse to
do so was strongest and ripest and most to be trusted,
never over-reaching himself or trifling imaginatively
with the poetic art, but stating only what he could vouch
for with every particle of his being, nay, with that fullness
and immediacy of nature that it was his genius to
rediscover in himself and make vocal again. Goethe
is the objective poet because the objective experience
—the desire for it, the search for it, the scrutiny of it
—is what he wrote about; it is his theme, his fable.
In the same sense Homer wrote of the Trojan Wars, and
may be called their poet.

Beyond this we cannot go, save to comment on the
mystery of personality which made this man and this
life and this poetry possible. If Goethe had not been
innately objective he would never have become the
objective poet. When Simmel said of him that he had
no metaphysic but that he was a metaphysic, he meant
exactly this. He meant that the clue to the difference
between Goethe and other men must be sought at a
metaphysical depth. The perplexity which the novice
in Goethe commonly finds—that of encountering a
personality which eludes all definition in terms of
idiosyncrasy and bias and yet remains incorrigibly
personal—cannot be resolved in any form of thought
less absolute than that of subject and object. Goethe's
genius for objective life, we discover, was as idiosyncratic
in him as the subjective idiosyncrasy in others. It was
born in him, and in developing it he was simply letting
himself go, finding himself, fulfilling himself in his own
way. His lyricism and the continual breaking of his
lyricism into non-lyrical forms—the central enigma in

his poetry—is the exact counterpart in literature of his unprecedented inner life.

This is the first and final mystery in Goethe. While other men are made to sit in Plato's cave with their faces to the wall, Goethe by some dispensation seems to sit sideways and to see both the wall and the objects which file past it. Of this unique vision—a vision at once abnormal and more than normal—his poetry is the record. All who seek to understand him must come to it, there is no alternative way of knowing him.

INDEX OF REFERENCES TO GOETHE'S WORKS

MADE AT THE
TEMPLE PRESS
LETCHWORTH
IN
GREAT BRITAIN